HOW TO MAKE YOURS

WINDY DRYDEN was born in
worked in psychotherapy and counselling for over 25
years, and is the author or editor of over 120 books,
including *How to Accept Yourself* (Sheldon Press, 1999)
and *Overcoming Anxiety* (Sheldon Press, 2000). Dr
Dryden is Professor of Counselling at Goldsmiths' Col-
lege, University of London.

Overcoming Common Problems Series

For a full list of titles please contact
Sheldon Press, Marylebone Road, London NW1 4DU

Overcoming Common Problems Series

Overcoming Common Problems Series

Overcoming Common Problems

How to Make Yourself Miserable

Dr Windy Dryden

First published in Great Britain in 2001
Sheldon Press, SPCK, Holy Trinity Church, Marylebone Road,
London NW1 4DU

British Library Cataloguing-in-Publication Data
A catalogue for this book is available from the British Library

ISBN 0–85969–917–3

Typeset by Deltatype Limited, Birkenhead, Merseyside
Printed in Great Britain by Biddles Ltd
www.biddles.co.uk

Contents

Introduction

I have written this book for those who are psychologically healthy and who wish to make themselves emotionally disturbed. You may be wondering why anyone would wish to choose emotional disturbance over psychological health. Let me let you into a secret. There are a number of advantages to be gained by being emotionally disturbed and a number of costs to being psychologically healthy. Let me list some of these respective payoffs and costs to show you what I mean.

Payoffs for being emotionally disturbed

- You get sympathy from people.
- People will help you out with a variety of tasks.
- You can get time off from work and still get paid.
- You may get early retirement on health grounds and get your pension paid early.
- People won't ask you to do difficult tasks.
- People won't put you under stress, so you will have an easier life.
- People won't have high expectations of you.
- You may be able to get people to do what you want them to do by reminding them verbally or by your actions that you suffer from emotional disturbance.
- Some people will look after you.
- If you are a student you may be able to get your degree without doing any work by dint of being emotionally disturbed (such a degree is called an aegrotat).
- If you fail at anything then you can put the blame on the fact that you were emotionally disturbed ('It wasn't me, it was my illness').

Costs of being psychologically healthy

- People will expect much of you and will be disappointed in you if you fail to live up to their expectations.
- You will be expected to carry the workload of others who are off

sick (including those who are away from work due to psychological problems).

- People will ask you to do onerous tasks because they think you are healthy enough to cope with them.
- You will get little sympathy from people if you show how emotionally healthy you are.
- People will expect you to look after them. They will certainly not want to look after you.
- Few people will offer to help you with things.
- If you do fail at anything you will not have anything or anyone to blame for this but yourself.
- People will not make allowances for you.

I hope you can see from the above that being emotionally disturbed leads to an easier life and being psychologically healthy leads to a much harder life. With this in mind, welcome to the world of emotional disturbance. This book will teach you how to make yourself emotionally disturbed in the first place and how to maintain your disturbance in the second place. Follow the steps that I outline in these pages and practise the skills that I teach. If your goal is to be emotionally disturbed, you won't be disappointed.

Windy Dryden

1

How to Make Yourself Anxious

Saying that you feel anxious is a great way of getting out of doing what you don't want to do. I used to work in a counselling service at a university, where many students who claimed that they had 'examination anxiety' were given permission to sit their exams in a small comfortable room with a friendly tutor instead of in a nasty, big, impersonal examination hall with officious bigwigs dressed up in their formal, frightening gowns.

Also, if you let it be known that you are an anxious person, people won't ask you to do things that you find stressful. This is particularly useful at work. Companies are now terrified of being sued for stressing out their employees, so your bosses will hardly risk stressing you if they can ask someone else less fragile. And if they don't promote you because you are fragile you can always threaten to sue them for discriminating against you. You can always go 'off sick' (a beautifully vague term that will come in very handy when the going gets tough for you at work) with the stress of being passed over.

So how do you make yourself anxious? By practising the following steps. While I will present them in the order in which I recommend you take them, you may vary the order until you find the one that leads you to feel most anxious. I will begin by giving you general advice concerning how to make yourself anxious, after which I will offer you more specific advice for making yourself anxious in specific areas.

General steps for making yourself anxious

Step 1: Understand that in order to feel anxious you need to think that you are about to face a threat

As I showed in my book *Overcoming Anxiety* (Sheldon Press, 2000) – which, of course you should under no circumstances read – in order to feel anxious you need to think that you are about to face some kind of threat. Remember this, for without threat you won't feel anxious.

1

There are two different kinds of threats that you may experience: threats to ego aspects of your personal domain, and threats to non-ego aspects of your personal domain. Now, your personal domain includes anything that you personally hold dear. So when you face an ego threat, you are facing a threat to something that you hold dear which has impact on your self-esteem (e.g. you think that you might fail an examination, knowing that if you did so you would consider yourself to be a failure). When you face a non-ego threat, you are facing a threat to something that you hold dear which does not have an impact on your self-esteem (e.g. you think that you might feel sick and you believe that you cannot bear experiencing such a feeling).

Now, I have two pieces of very good news for you. First, the world is full of threat, so you won't have to look too far to find a threat about which you can make yourself anxious. Second, you can make yourself anxious about imagined threats, so the threats don't have to be real. As long as you think that they are about to happen, that will do it. So, in the unlikely event that you can't find something threatening in your life (and if you do find it a struggle to find something threatening, you are a tough customer and will need to read this chapter many times to get the anxiety habit), you can always think, for example, that a Goodyear air balloon will explode over your head and burn your house down, and that will do the trick. If anybody were to tell you that this is very unlikely to occur, here's a good way to shut them up. Just ask them for an absolute guarantee that this will not occur – that should do it.

So there is really little point in saying that you couldn't make yourself anxious because you could not find anything threatening in your life. I will give you more guidance on this point when I come to Step 3.

Step 2: Practise a general anxiety-creating philosophy (GAP)

While locating a threat is a necessary condition for you to feel anxious, sadly it is not sufficient for you to feel anxious. Some people, for example, feel concerned rather than anxious about the possibility of facing a threat. Avoid such people like the plague, by the way, because they may interfere with you learning how to make yourself anxious. No, unfortunately you need what I call a 'general anxiety-creating philosophy' (GAP) to ensure that you will feel anxious about the real and imagined threats in your life.

There are four components to such a philosophy, and in my experience you will need two of the four to ensure that you will become anxious. Let me review these components one at a time.

1   A rigid demand

When you hold a rigid demand about threats, you assert that these threats must not exist. For example, identify a category of events that you are generally anxious about – e.g. going for a health check – and identify the threat in that category – e.g. discovering that you are ill. When you hold a rigid demand, you insist that you must not be ill. By demanding that something which may occur absolutely must not occur, you achieve the following:

- First, you give yourself the feeling of anxiety, so the demand works!
- Second, you make yourself so preoccupied with the possibility that you are ill that you exclude the possibility that you may be well, and all you can think about concerns illness. Thus, you give yourself tunnel vision that will help to sustain your anxiety.
- Third, you will increase your chances of avoiding going for health checks. This will have the effect of reinforcing the idea that it would be absolutely horrible to be ill. If it wasn't horrible, you reason, you wouldn't avoid going for health checks.

Rigid demands would make sense if they actually removed the possibility of facing a threat. Thus, if by demanding that you must not be ill you removed the possibility of being ill, then making this demand would make sense. However, making demands has no such effect on reality. It doesn't magically remove the possibility of threats existing. But don't let such considerations influence you, since, don't forget, your goal is to be anxious. Consequently, you don't want to make sense in case doing so interferes with your quest to make yourself anxious.

2   An awfulizing belief

Another very good way of making yourself anxious is to believe that it would be horrible, awful, terrible or the end of the world for the threat to exist in the first place and for it to occur in the second place. This is known as holding an awfulizing belief, and for it to work you have to convert your sensible, non-extreme conclusions – such as that it would be bad or unfortunate to be ill – into illogical extreme conclusions – such as that it would be absolutely dreadful or the end of the world to be ill.

If you are struggling to keep hold of an awfulizing belief, the following additional advice may be of some assistance. When you think of going for health checks, for example, tell yourself that if you were discovered to be ill, nothing could be worse than this, and if it did happen, absolutely no good could possibly come from such an eventuality. That should do the trick.

3 A low frustration tolerance belief

The third component of your general anxiety-creating philosophy (GAP) is known as a low frustration tolerance (LFT) belief. Here, you strongly show yourself that you wouldn't be able to bear or tolerate it if the threat were to materialize. For example, telling yourself that it would be intolerable for you to be ill would help quite a lot to get your anxiety juices flowing. Again, if you find this difficult you might find it helpful to picture yourself crumpled up in a heap on being told that you are ill, or to show yourself that you would lose your capacity for happiness if you were ill.

4 A self-depreciation belief

As I mentioned above, there are two basic forms of anxiety: ego anxiety, where you make yourself anxious about a threat to your self-esteem, and non-ego anxiety, where you make yourself anxious about threats other than to your self-esteem. In the latter type of anxiety – non-ego anxiety – you generally hold a rigid demand, and then either an awfulizing belief is most dominant in your thinking or an LFT belief is. Putting this diagrammatically we have:

> Non-ego anxiety = Threat to non-ego aspect of personal domain x rigid demand + awfulizing belief

or

> Non-ego anxiety = Threat to non-ego aspect of personal domain x rigid demand + LFT belief

In ego anxiety, on the other hand, you generally hold a rigid demand and a self-depreciation belief, as shown below:

Ego anxiety = Threat to ego aspect of personal domain x rigid demand + self-depreciation belief

When you hold a self-depreciation belief, you make a global negative rating, judgement or evaluation about your entire self (e.g. 'I am a failure', 'I am less worthy', 'I am unlovable').

For example, identify a category of events that you are anxious about, which if they happened would result in you lowering your self-esteem, such as being disapproved of. This is an ego threat. Now add your rigid demand and self-depreciation to this threat and we have: 'I must not be disapproved of, and if I am this proves that I am an unlikeable person.'

You now have a powerful recipe for inducing anxiety. Practise your general anxiety-creating philosophy until you really believe it. Once you have truly internalized it, you are ready for the next stage.

Step 3: Focus on a specific threat and practise a specific version of your general anxiety-creating philosophy

One of the advantages of holding a general anxiety-creating philosophy (GAP) is that it increases the chances of identifying threats in your environment. This ability to locate threats to your personal domain is very important if you are to become really good at making yourself anxious. If you only identified such threats when they actually existed, you could still make yourself anxious but you wouldn't do so very often. To make yourself anxious regularly and frequently, it is important for you to become very sensitive to threats to your personal domain. This is where GAPs become very handy, in that they sensitize you to the possibility of threat in the absence of objective evidence that such threats actually exist.

Let me explain how holding a GAP influences your ability to identify threats in your environment, before listing common GAPs which, once internalized, will lead to a lifetime of anxiety.

Let's suppose that you hold the following GAP: 'I must be approved by new people that I meet and if I'm not it proves that I am unlikeable.' If you believe this, then unless you are certain that new people will like you when you meet them (and who can be certain of that?), you will become preoccupied with the possibility that they will not like you and will think that you are unlikeable. This preoccupation will involve you in doing the following:

1 It involves you overestimating the chances that a new group of people won't approve of you and underestimating the chances that they will approve of you.
(**Overestimating the *probability* of disapproval**)
2 It also involves you thinking that if they do disapprove of you they will disapprove of you greatly, rather than just mildly or moderately.
(**Overestimating the *degree* of disapproval**)
3 It further involves you thinking that all or most of those present will disapprove of you, rather than the more realistic situation where some might disapprove of you, others might approve of you and yet others might be neutral towards you – assuming that you don't have crass social habits which will objectively antagonize all or most of the people you have just met.
(**Overestimating the *extent* of disapproval**)

In summary, let me put it like this: when you hold a GAP about approval, for example, you will overestimate the probability, degree and extent of the opposite happening (i.e. being disapproved of) in your environment. GAPs lead you to become oversensitive to threat, which is exactly what you need to develop and maintain an anxiety problem.

So far I have discussed the role that general anxiety-creating philosophies play in making you oversensitive to threat in your environment. Once you have identified a specific threat in a specific environment you need to evaluate that threat in a specific way so that you can keep your anxiety alive. To do this you need to hold a specific version of your GAP. For example, let's suppose that you hold the GAP I discussed above, namely: 'I must be approved by new people that I meet and if I'm not it proves that I am unlikeable.' Now, let's further assume that you go to a party where there are people that you don't know and your host is about to introduce you to these people. Your GAP will immediately lead you to focus on the threat in this situation for you, e.g. that these specific people will not like you. This is known as an inference. An inference is a hunch about reality that can be correct or incorrect, but your GAP leads you to think of it as a fact.

Having focused on this specific threat, you need to evaluate it using a specific version of your GAP. In this case, it is: 'These people that I am about to meet must not disapprove of me, and if they do it means that I am unlikeable.' Holding this specific belief and applying it to the threat-related inference will mean that you will be anxious in the specific situation under consideration.

So if you want to be anxious in specific situations, focus on specific threats in the situation (your relevant GAPs will be especially valuable in helping you to do this) and then evaluate these specific threats using specific irrational beliefs (which may well be specific versions of relevant GAPs).

Step 4: Focus on and go with the consequences of taking Step 3

Congratulations! You now know how to seek out threats in your environment (by developing GAPs) and you know how to make yourself anxious about these threats by evaluating them with specific versions of your GAPs. This feeling of anxiety, then, is the emotional consequence of this threat–irrational belief interaction, as shown below:

Specific threat x specific irrational belief = emotional consequence
ANXIETY

However, there are two other consequences of this threat–irrational belief interaction which are very useful in both maintaining and exacerbating your anxiety. These are known as behavioural consequences and thinking consequences.

Behavioural consequences

Let's start with the behavioural consequences of the threat x irrational belief interaction. Thus, when you think that new people you are about to meet will disapprove of you (threat) and you demand that this must not happen and that you are unlikeable if it does (irrational belief) then you will act or tend to act in a number of ways:

- You will tend to avoid meeting these new people.
  (**Avoiding the threat**)
- If you have to meet these new people, you will leave at the first opportunity.
  (**Physically withdrawing from the threat**)

7

- If you can't leave the situation you will remain silent so that you don't do anything to provoke disapproval. (**Passive neutralizing of the threat**)
- You go out of your way to get approval from the people concerned. (**Active neutralizing of the threat**)
- If you can't leave the situation you will find some way of behaviourally distracting yourself from the threat, such as picking your hands. (**Behavioural distraction from the threat**)
- You may try and deal with the threat by overcompensating for it (e.g. by actively provoking disapproval to try to convince yourself that you don't care whether you are approved or not). (**Behaviourally overcompensating for the threat**)

If you wish to maintain your anxiety once you have created it, then it is important that you act in one or more of the above ways. When you do act in such ways you are actually rehearsing and thus strengthening your specific and general irrational beliefs. Thus, when you avoid being introduced to a new group of people you do so because implicitly you think something like: 'If I were to meet these people, they might disapprove of me. They must not disapprove of me, and if they do it means that I am unlikeable. Therefore, I'll avoid meeting them.' And when you strengthen your irrational beliefs about threat, you increase the likelihood that you will make yourself anxious in future.

The following sums up what I have said in this section:

Specific threat x specific irrational belief =	Behavioural consequences
	1 AVOIDING THE THREAT
	2 PHYSICALLY WITHDRAWING FROM THE THREAT
	3 PASSIVE NEUTRALIZING OF THE THREAT
	4 ACTIVE NEUTRALIZING OF THE THREAT
	5 BEHAVIOURAL DISTRACTION FROM THE THREAT
	6 BEHAVIOURALLY OVERCOMPENSATING FOR THE THREAT

Thinking consequences

There are also thinking consequences of the threat x irrational belief interaction. These consequences are of two types. The first type involves you elaborating on the threat. For example, when you think that new people you are about to meet will disapprove of you (threat) and you demand that this must not happen and you are unlikeable if it does (irrational belief) then you will tend to think in a number of ways:

- You will tend to think that the consequences of the disapproval that you predict you will receive will be highly negative. Thus, you may think that once the strangers disapprove of you then they will tell others about their negative views of you, that their disapproval of you will last a long time and that it may affect your chances of meeting new friends in the future.
  (**Exaggerating the negative consequences of the predicted threat**)

This thinking consequence serves to increase your anxiety because it gives you even more negative threats to think about and evaluate with other specific irrational beliefs. As such you should strive hard to become adept at this skill.

The other type of thinking consequence involves you trying to deal with the threat in a number of (ineffective) ways:

- You try to distract yourself from the threat by attempting to think of something else.
  (**Cognitive distraction from the threat**)
- You attempt to overcompensate for the threat in your thinking by either imagining yourself being indifferent to the disapproval or thinking of yourself gaining great approval in another (imaginary) setting.
  (**Cognitively overcompensating for the threat**)

These two thinking consequences serve to maintain your anxiety in ways that are similar to the behavioural consequences I discussed earlier, in that they implicitly give you an opportunity to rehearse and thus strengthen your irrational belief. Thus, if you try to distract yourself from the possibility that a new group of people will not approve of you, you are largely doing so because you believe that they must approve of you and you are unlikeable if they don't. If you weren't evaluating the threat in this anxiety-creating way, you would be more likely to think about the threat objectively, and to deal with it constructively if it actually occurred. Since you don't want to do that, my advice is to engage in both cognitive distraction and cognitive overcompensation whenever you want a break from thinking about the exaggerated negative consequences of the threat, which is the more productive of the thinking consequences that I have discussed in deepening your anxiety.

To sum up:

Specific threat x specific irrational belief =	thinking consequences
	1 EXAGGERATING THE NEGATIVE CONSEQUENCES OF THE PREDICTED THREAT
	2 COGNITIVE DISTRACTION FROM THE THREAT
	3 COGNITIVELY OVERCOMPENSATING FOR THE THREAT

Step 5: Keep increasing your anxiety

If you have followed the above four steps and practised well what I have advised, you should by now be quite adept at making yourself anxious. However, to become a black belt at anxiety you need to know how to keep increasing your anxiety. To do this you have to evaluate every aspect of your anxiety with a specific anxiety-creating belief so that your anxiety builds and builds. Let me give you an example of what I mean.

Let's assume again that you have the following GAP: 'I must be approved by new people that I meet and if I'm not it proves that I am unlikeable', and that you are attending a social gathering where you are likely to be introduced to people that you don't know. Under these conditions, your GAP will lead you to identify a specific threat in this situation, namely that strangers at the gathering are likely to disapprove of you. You then evaluate this specific threat with a specific version of your GAP until you have made yourself anxious. Then – and this is the important point – focus on some aspect of your anxiety and evaluate this using another specific anxiety-creating irrational belief. Here are some examples of how to increase your anxiety in this way:

- *Focus on your feelings of anxiety* and tell yourself: 'I must not be anxious, I can't stand feeling anxious and I have to get rid of it immediately.' This will increase your feelings of anxiety.
- *Focus on a symptom of your anxiety* (such as your heart pounding) and tell yourself: 'I must stop my heart pounding and it will be terrible if I don't.' This will increase your heart pounding and also make it more likely that you will think that you will have a heart attack if your palpitations increase – which they will if you hold such a belief.
- *Focus on a behavioural consequence of your anxiety* (e.g. your urge to avoid meeting new people) and tell yourself: 'I must not feel like avoiding this situation and because I do I am a weak wimp.'
- *Focus on a thinking consequence of your anxiety* (e.g. that new people will laugh at you if you say something silly) and tell yourself: 'New people must not laugh at me and if they do it proves that I am an utter fool.'

As you keep increasing your feelings of anxiety, your negative thoughts will become more dire and your urge to act in unconstructive ways will become more pressing. When this happens, evaluate each spiral with another anxiety-creating belief until you are in a state of panic, your thoughts are spiralling out of control and your behaviour is equally chaotic. If you follow these guidelines and practise them rigorously, you will soon have an anxiety problem that will be hard to treat.

How to make yourself anxious about losing self-control

One of the common themes in people's anxiety about themselves concerns losing self-control. This is not surprising, since one of the things many of us take pride in is our ability to remain in control of ourselves and, in particular, of our feelings, our thoughts and our behaviour. Now, if you want to make yourself anxious about losing self-control you need to hold a rigid demand about self-control in the area of your preoccupation. For example:

- 'I must not feel anxious (loss of self-control of feelings).'
- 'I must not think weird thoughts (loss of self-control of thoughts).'
- 'I must not have images that I find hard to dismiss (loss of self-control of images).'
- 'I must not have the urge to act in that way (loss of self-control over urges to act).'
- 'I must not behave in a certain way (loss of self-control over behaviour).'

Once you have practised these rigid demands, bring a relevant demand to an episode where you have begun to lose a bit of self-control. For example, imagine that you have begun to have an image of throwing yourself off a bridge. Tell yourself that you must not have such a mental picture and that you must get rid of the image immediately. What will happen is that the image will become stronger and it will increase in aversiveness. Next, you may begin to think that unless you gain control of your images right now – as, of course, you must – then you will go mad. You will then tend to avoid situations with which you associate losing control. Thus you may well avoid going over bridges if you have had the image of throwing yourself off a bridge. You may also avoid the subject of mental breakdown and pictures of psychiatric hospitals in an attempt to regain emotional control, but as you do so you unwittingly increase your dire need for self-control. After a while you will quickly jump in your mind from the beginning of losing self-control (e.g. beginning to have the image of throwing yourself off a bridge) to the end, where you have gone crazy. What will help you in making this leap is the idea that I suggest you practise three times a day: 'Either I am in perfect control of my psychological processes or they will run riot far beyond my capability to control them and I will soon go mad.'

Another aspect of this that will add to your anxiety about losing self-control is the idea that your thoughts, feelings and urges to act are a good guide to reality – for instance, if you think that you are going to throw yourself off a bridge then you will. If you believe this then it won't be difficult for you to feel anxious. Since you think that having the image of throwing yourself off a bridge means that you are going to do it, in order to make yourself safe you think that you mustn't have such an image. Paradoxically, when you demand that you must not have a thought or an image, then you make it more likely that you will have such a thought or image. With every intensification of the image, redouble your demands to get rid of the image, and soon all you will be able to think of is throwing yourself off a bridge. Having done this, take the following steps:

- *Avoid actual bridges* This shouldn't be difficult, since if you believe that thinking you will throw yourself off a bridge means that you are going to do it, the last thing you are going to do is to walk over a bridge. Although taking this step may seem as if you are avoiding feelings of anxiety, what you are actually doing is strengthening your anxiety-creating belief. In effect, you are saying something along the lines of: 'I must avoid seeing a bridge, and if I do see one then I will have the image of throwing myself off the bridge – and that's terrible, for if I think the thought, I will do the deed.'
- *Avoid pictures of bridges*. Again, taking this step may seem like avoiding anxiety, but as I have discussed above, such avoidance actually strengthens your anxiety-creating belief. Thus, if your avoidance could talk it would say: 'I must not see a picture of a bridge, and if I do see one it will remind me of a real bridge. Being reminded of the real thing will lead me to think of throwing myself off the bridge – and that's terrible, for if I think the thought then I will do the deed.'

The above two situations show that, far from helping you to deal with your anxiety, avoidance helps you to strengthen your anxiety-creating beliefs and thus renders you vulnerable to feeling anxiety, which is exactly what you want to do.

How to make yourself anxious about uncertainty

Many people make themselves anxious about uncertainty. In case you don't know how to do this, here is what you do:

1 Focus on something uncertain which constitutes a threat to you (e.g. 'My children are 15 minutes late home and I don't know what has happened to them').
2 Rehearse the belief that you must be sure that the threat does

not exist and that it is awful not to have such certainty (e.g. 'I must know that my children are safe and it is awful not to know this').

3 Practise the idea that uncertainty means that bad things will inevitably occur (e.g. 'Because I don't know that my children are safe and I must know this, not knowing that they are safe means that something bad has happened to them').

4 Rehearse your awfulizing belief about their occurrence (e.g. 'It would be awful if my children were not safe').

5 Seek reassurance from others that the threat really does not exist or keep checking to determine that the threat does not exist (e.g. 'I keep going to the window to check whether I can see them and I ring round their friends to discover whether they know about my children's whereabouts').

6 Cast doubt on such reassurance ('When the parents of my children's friends try to reassure me that my children are OK I am immediately reassured, but then I doubt this, saying such things to myself as "How do they know?", "They are only saying this to reassure me", "I'm sure that they would be out of their minds with worry if it was their children who were late"').

7 Re-rehearse your awfulizing belief about the occurrence of the bad things listed in Step 4 ('It would be awful if my children were not safe').

8 Keep repeating Steps 5–7.

9 Keep a scrapbook of stories about the bad things that happen to children who are late home, and ignore the millions of unreported incidents of children being late home who were safe.

10 When people try to reassure you that it is very unlikely that anything really bad has happened to your children, remind yourself that 'unlikely' means that there still is a small chance, and demand to know that this small chance does not apply to your children. By insisting that you have to know 100 per cent that your children are safe, you will focus on the fact that since you don't know they are safe, they must be at risk.

How to become socially anxious

When you are socially anxious, you experience the distinct advantage that many people will give you a wide berth. As a result you are spared meeting people who are very boring, and you do not develop friendships with people who may well use you. So here is how to become socially anxious:

1 When you get to a relevant social situation, remember your ideal social behaviour and focus on how you will fall far short of such behaviour. Demand that you must act in accord with your ideal and that you are a worthless person if you don't.
2 Think that others present will judge you negatively, but don't look at them so that you can't disconfirm this inference.
3 While thinking that others are judging you negatively, demand that they must not do this, and that if they do this proves that you are worthless.
4 Avoid similar social situations in future, but in your avoidant state keep reminding yourself that if you do go out socially you must come across well and you must be liked, otherwise you will be worthless.
5 Develop poor social skills. Do not engage people in appropriate eye contact. Either stare at people for a long period of time or do not engage in eye contact with them at all.
6 Develop a good repertoire of inappropriate social behaviour. For example, change the subject at inopportune times, interrupt other people and make critical remarks about people to their face. These inappropriate social behaviours will encourage people to dislike you, and when they do you can practise depreciating yourself as a worthless person.

How to develop hypochondria

Hypochondria is the condition where you think that you have a serious illness in the absence of convincing evidence to support your contention. In order to develop this condition, which will get you a lot of attention from the medical profession, you have to follow a number of simple steps.

1 Practise the general irrational belief that you must know at all times that you don't have a serious disease and that it is terrible if you don't have such certainty. This belief will help you to become adept at identifying symptoms that could be signs of serious illness.
2 Focus on a particular symptom that could be evidence of a serious

illness (skin blemishes, lumps and pains are particularly good, but any symptom will do). In this section I will assume that you have identified a pain in your chest. Practise a specific version of the above-mentioned general irrational belief (e.g. 'I must know now that this chest pain is not a sign of a heart attack and I can't bear not knowing this').

3 Practise the thought that uncertainty in this context is a sign of serious illness.

4 Seek professional advice, and when it is given and you are reassured that there is nothing seriously wrong with you, cast doubt on this reassurance when your symptom persists. In this context, it is very important that you disbelieve the view that states that the continuation of your symptom is due to the attention that you give to it, influenced as it is by your irrational belief. Rather, it is important that you accept the view that such symptoms are exclusively due to organic, non-psychological symptoms.

Good ways to cast doubt on the validity of the medical opinion that you have been given that there is nothing wrong with you include:

- Doubt the thoroughness of the examination (e.g. 'In retrospect the doctor only gave me a cursory examination and he (in this case) didn't ask me many questions about my symptoms. I really think that he missed something').
- Doubt the state of the medical examiner when she (in this case) conducted the examination (e.g. 'Come to think of it, the doctor looked pale and distracted when she was examining me. I really think that she missed something').
- Doubt the competence of the medical examiner (e.g. 'I've heard a number of people say that the doctor who examined me is incompetent. I really think that he missed something').

5 Consult another medical examiner, and once again cast doubt on the opinion that you are given, following the same points discussed in the above section, if she (in this case) examines you and can't find anything wrong. Keep repeating the points above for every medical examiner that you consult.

6 Ask others for reassurance. Family and friends are good sources for reassurance and they are usually happy, at least initially, to give this to you on the basis that they think they are helping you

(they are not) or that they can't bear to see you upset (when they can).

7 Consult books on medical symptoms and visit sites on the World Wide Web in the hope of finding out that your symptoms are benign. However, you will inevitably find something to support the view that you are seriously ill, and when you find such information accept it as true, at least in your case.

8 Keep checking to determine the status of the symptom. This will increase your hypochondria in two ways. First, checking will focus your attention on the symptom that you are worried about and will mean that you will be more aware of it, and your increased attention will lead to an intensification of your symptoms. As you think that your symptoms are getting worse, you awfulize about this situation, which will lead you to conclude that you must be seriously ill. Second, there are symptoms such as skin blemishes and lumps that get worse if you physically check on them by touching them. Once again, if you awfulize about this 'deterioration', you will tend to conclude that you are seriously ill.

9 Act as though you are seriously ill. Thus, if you think that the chest pains you have been experiencing mean that you are suffering from a heart condition, act accordingly. For example, don't do too much exercise and avoid strenuous exercise that might put a strain on your heart.

How to have a panic attack

Panic attacks are particularly painful and therefore very valuable for people who wish to develop and maintain anxiety. There are three core elements of a panic attack that are important for you to learn, digest and practise:

• the belief that you must not lose control and it is terrible if you do;
• the notion that when your symptoms increase, this is evidence that you are facing an imminent internal catastrophe (e.g. a heart attack, a stroke, going mad, fainting, to name but a few);
• the idea that it is terrible to have a panic attack and that you must avoid doing so at any costs.

Let's take these points one at a time.

1 In order to lay the foundations of a panic attack, you need to acquire and practise an 'anxiety about anxiety' philosophy. Let's

suppose that you are waiting to give a public presentation and you notice that you feel somewhat anxious and sweaty. When you tell yourself that it is horrific to feel anxious and that you must gain control of it immediately, you then increase your anxiety. If every time your anxiety increases you awfulize about it, then you will begin to feel that you are really losing control. When you get to this stage it will be very easy for you to demand that you must gain control immediately and that it will be terrible if you don't.

2 At this point it is important that you infer that an immediate, catastrophic internal event is likely to happen. As discussed above, common catastrophic inferences include having a heart attack, having a stroke, going mad in some way. Then you have to act in order to avoid such an event happening. For example, if you think that you are going to have a stroke, you may sit down. In doing so, you may calm down because you think that your action has warded off having a stroke. In this way, you never actually test out the validity of your inference, something you don't want to do if you want to keep having panic attacks.

3 The final step is for you to become anxious about having a panic attack. In order to do this you need to do three things:

- Practise the belief that you must not experience a panic attack and it would be awful to do so.
- Wherever you go, think that you might have a panic attack and practise the above belief.
- Avoid going to places where you think that you might have a panic attack.

If, after all this, you still find it difficult to have a panic attack, you might find it helpful to bring on very uncomfortable symptoms and then take the three steps outlined above. Thus, you could breathe through a straw or engage in rapid shallow breathing until, for example, you hyperventilate, feel faint and think that you might pass out.

Develop and rehearse a view of the world founded on anxiety-creating irrational beliefs

People develop views of the world as it relates to them that render them vulnerable to particular unhealthy negative emotions. This is certainly the case with anxiety. The world views that render you vulnerable to anxiety do so primarily because they make it very easy for you to make anxiety-related inferences. You then make yourself anxious about these inferences with the appropriate irrational beliefs. Here is an illustrative list of world views for you to develop and rehearse, together with the inferences that they spawn.

World view: The world is a dangerous place

Inference: If a situation can be threatening then it is threatening.

World view: Uncertainty is dangerous

Inference: Not knowing that a threat does not exist means that it does.

World view: Not being in control is dangerous

Inference: If I am not in control then I will soon lose control completely.

World view: People can't be trusted

Inference: People are unpredictable and will threaten me without warning.

I hope you can see how you can become really adept at creating anxiety for yourself. I will now move on to teach you how to become really adept at making yourself feel depressed.

2

How to Make Yourself Depressed

As with anxiety, when you are depressed people are unlikely to ask you to do something that is stressful for you to do. Thus, if you play your cards right and involve people in your life who would be too upset to do anything to deepen your depression, you can live a fairly stress-free life. Being depressed also elicits sympathy and concern from other people (at least initially).

So what characterizes those people who will protect you from the rigours of the world and show ongoing concern for your welfare when you are depressed? Such people are largely selfless people whose self-esteem is based on helping others. And who could be more deserving of such help than you, with your depression? Also, such people have a guilt problem and the idea that they would put their desires before your own is ludicrous. If you want to get most mileage from others when you are depressed, choose people who are selfless and who have problems with guilt.

How do you make yourself depressed? Let me begin our discussion this time with some advice about preparing the ground for depression to take root.

Preparing the ground for depression

Depression is very much experienced physically, and therefore in order for you to feel depressed it is a good idea to prepare the ground so that your depressed feelings can take root. Consequently, I suggest that you take the following advice.

- Don't wash, and walk around all day wearing only your pyjamas/ nightgown.
- Read only the bad news in daily newspapers.
- Play as many songs written by Leonard Cohen as you can find.
- Withdraw from any events that you are likely to enjoy. Only attend events where there is a very good chance of feeling depressed, either during the event or after it is finished. Even if you do enjoy the event, point out to yourself that you used to enjoy such events a lot more.

21

- Do things that you are likely to fail at and avoid doings things where you are likely to be successful. If you do succeed at anything, point out to yourself that you used to do such things much better than you do now, and/or that if you could do it then anybody could do it.

How to make yourself depressed: sociotropic depression

It is useful to distinguish between two types of depression: sociotropic depression and autonomous depression. In sociotropic depression you are depressed about issues such as loss of affiliation, loss of love, loss of being connected to people and loss of relationships, whereas in autonomous depression you are depressed about losses of freedom, autonomy, competence and status. In this section I will show you how to make yourself sociotropically depressed, while in the next section I will concentrate on showing you how to make yourself autonomously depressed.

Making yourself sociotropically depressed: the role of general irrational beliefs

In order to make yourself sociotropically depressed you have to hold a number of general irrational beliefs.

1 First, you need to hold a *rigid demand* about the place of being liked, loved and connected to people in your life, and the role that relationships play for you. For example:

- 'I must be liked.'
- 'I must be loved.'
- 'I must be connected to people that I care for.'
- 'I must have a special relationship in my life.'

2 Second, in some forms of sociotropic depression you need to hold a *self-depreciation* belief about these issues. I call this type of depression 'self-worth sociotropic depression' because in effect you are basing your self-esteem on the presence of being liked, loved, etc. For example:

- '(I must be liked) . . . and if I'm not, then I'm unlikeable.'
- '(I must be loved) . . . and if I'm not, then I'm unlovable.'

- '(I must be connected to people that I care for) . . . and if I'm not then I am not worth caring about.'
- '(I must have a special relationship in my life) . . . and if I don't then I'm a nobody.'

3 Third, in other forms of sociotropic depression (which I call 'non-self-worth sociotropic depression'), you are not depreciating yourself. Rather, you are disturbing yourself about the resultant conditions that exist following your loss. Some of these beliefs demonstrate dependency. For example:

- '(I must be liked) . . . and if I'm not, I couldn't bear it.'
- '(I must be loved) . . . and if I'm not, it's awful.'
- '(I must be connected to people that I care for) . . . and if I'm not then I would disintegrate since I am too weak to look after myself.'
- '(I must have a special relationship in my life) . . . and if I'm not my life is nothing.'

Making yourself sociotropically depressed: seek out loss in your mind

Once you have practised your general irrational beliefs about loss with respect to being liked, loved, etc., the next step is to focus on this loss in your mind. It is important to make this loss as specific as possible. Thus, your specific loss can be a past loss, where you recall a specific time when you were or thought you were rejected, disliked or disconnected. Or alternatively, you can review your present relationships and focus on one which isn't going too well; evaluate this relationship with a relevant irrational belief, as detailed above, until you conclude that the other person doesn't like you, doesn't love you or wants to reject you.

Making yourself sociotropically depressed: evaluate your specific loss with a specific irrational belief

Once you have focused on a loss, the next step is to evaluate it using a specific version of your general irrational belief. Thus, let's suppose that you have identified a recent situation where you thought Rosemary, a friend, has acted coolly towards you. Using your general irrational belief – 'My friends must always show interest in me and if they do not, it proves that I am an unlikeable person' – you translate this 'cool action' into the inference that your friend has rejected you. Focusing on this specific loss, evaluate it with a specific version of your general belief, namely: 'Rosemary must not reject me and because she did, I am an unlikeable person.'

Making yourself sociotropically depressed: act depressed

Now that you feel depressed about a specific loss, it is important that you maintain and even deepen that depression by your behaviour. In other words, it is important that you act in ways that are consistent with your depressed mood. Returning to our example, experiment with the following to see which deepens your depression:

- Avoid Rosemary and other friends.
- Stay away from enjoyable activities.
- Play depressing music, or read depressing novels or poetry (particularly those that deal with rejection).
- Talk to people who are also depressed.

Making yourself sociotropically depressed: think depressed

One important result of depression-related irrational beliefs is that they have a decided negative effect on your subsequent thinking. This information is very useful if you want to become really proficient at depressing yourself. Let me outline and exemplify some of the thinking errors that *stem from* or *follow from* your specific irrational belief that 'Rosemary must not reject me and because she did, I am an unlikeable person'. These thinking errors will help you to deepen your depression:

- **Black and white thinking** (taking an event and putting it into one of two black and white categories): 'You either like me or you dislike me. There is no other way of looking at it. Since Rosemary has rejected me on this occasion, this means that she doesn't like me.'
- **Overgeneralization** (taking an event and generalizing it to all other similar situations and relevant categories): 'Since Rosemary rejected me, all my friends will reject me.'
- **Always–never thinking** (taking an event and thinking that it will be like this for ever or it will never change): 'I'll never be friends with Rosemary again. I'll always be rejected by my friends.'
- **Exaggeration** (using an event as a springboard to make extreme and exaggerated statements about it and matters relating to it): 'Nobody truly likes me.'

24

- **Negative prediction** (taking an event and making negative predictions about it and matters relating to it): 'Whoever I make friends with in the future will reject me.'
- **Ignoring the positive** (making one event colour everything in your life so that you ignore the positive): 'The fact that I got a good review at work doesn't matter. The only thing that matters is that Rosemary has rejected me.'
- **Helplessness** (editing out your personal resourcefulness to change matters on a broad scale): 'I can't do anything to get people to like me. They are capable of liking me, but I don't have the resources of getting them to like me.'
- **Hopelessness** (seeing no hope for the future): 'No matter what happens, I'll be emotionally alone in the future. I have the resources to change matters, but they just can't be changed.'

If you find yourself correcting these errors, go back and rehearse your original specific irrational belief. Doing so will then help you to return to making your thinking errors and will help you to sustain your feelings of depression.

A particularly potent combination of thinking errors in the deepening of depression is helplessness and hopelessness. In this context, show yourself that you don't have the resources to get people to like you (helplessness) and that even if you did it wouldn't change anything (hopelessness).

Making yourself sociotropically depressed: evaluate your subsequent negative thinking with irrational beliefs, and keep doing this until you feel hopeless

Once you have created a particular thinking error by evaluating your loss with a specific irrational depression-creating belief, you then have a glorious opportunity to make yourself even more depressed, so do not spurn it. What you do is to focus on the content of your thinking error and evaluate this with another specific irrational belief. For example, imagine that you have created the following thinking error and are now focusing on it: 'Whoever I make friends with in the future will reject me.' Now evaluate this with the following irrational belief: 'People must not keep rejecting me, and if they do it proves that I am completely worthless.'

What will in all probability happen is that your subsequent thinking will be even more negative and distorted (e.g. 'I will always be alone. I will never be connected to another human being again. Life will always be bleak and hopeless'). You will notice that you are now feeling hopeless about the future. That's great, because you have now achieved your goal: to be well and truly depressed. Just to be on the safe side, I suggest that you implement some or all of the strategies I listed at the beginning of this chapter under the section entitled 'Preparing the ground for depression'. This will keep you in your hopeless frame of mind.

Making yourself sociotropically depressed: use metaphors and images

Although you probably won't need to do so, because you will now be in a hopeless frame of mind, I suggest that you create and dwell on images or metaphors that illustrate how you feel. Here are a few suggestions that depict the hopelessness of sociotropic depression:

- 'I am in solitary isolation with no way out.'
- 'I see others enjoying themselves and I have no way of reaching them, I am in a glass jar.'
- 'I am trapped in a loveless existence.'

If you rehearse such metaphors and images then you will maintain and even deepen your sense of hopelessness.

How to make yourself depressed: autonomous depression

As I pointed out earlier in this chapter, there are two types of depression: sociotropic depression and autonomous depression. If you recall, in sociotropic depression you are depressed about issues such as loss of affiliation, loss of love, loss of being connected to people and loss of relationships, whereas in autonomous depression you are depressed about losses of freedom, autonomy, competence and status. In this section, I will show you how to make yourself autonomously depressed.

Making yourself autonomously depressed: the role of general irrational beliefs

In order to make yourself autonomously depressed you have to hold a number of general irrational beliefs.

1 First, you need to hold a *rigid demand* about the place of key goals and standards in your life such as achievement, competence, self-reliance, being autonomous and having high status. For example:

- 'I must achieve what I want in life.'
- 'I must be competent.'
- 'I must be able to determine my life path free from external restrictions.'
- 'I must be self-reliant.'
- 'I must achieve the status in life that I have set for myself.'

2 Second, in some forms of autonomous depression you need to hold a *self-depreciation belief* about these issues. I call this type of depression 'self-worth autonomous depression' because in effect you are basing your self-esteem on the presence of conditions such as achievement, competence, self-reliance, autonomy and status.

- '(I must achieve what I want in life) . . . and if I don't then I am a failure.'
- '(I must be competent) . . . and if I'm not then I am an idiot.'
- '(I must be able to determine my life path free from external restrictions) . . . and if I can't then I am a useless person.'
- '(I must be self-reliant) . . . and if I'm not then I am a weak person.'
- '(I must achieve the status in life that I set for myself) . . . and if I don't then I am worthless.'

3 Third, in other forms of autonomy depression (which I call 'non-self-worth autonomous depression'), you are not depreciating yourself. Rather, you are disturbing yourself about the resultant conditions that exist following your loss.

- '(I must achieve what I want in life) . . . and if I don't, I couldn't bear it.'
- '(I must be competent) . . . and if I'm not, it's awful.'
- '(I must be able to determine my life path free from external restrictions) . . . and if I am not able to, it's intolerable.'

- '(I must be self-reliant) . . . and it's the end of the world if I'm not.'
- '(I must achieve the status in life that I have set for myself) . . . and if I don't, I couldn't stand it.'

Making yourself autonomously depressed: seek out loss in your mind

Once you have practised your general irrational beliefs about loss to your personal domain in the area of autonomy, etc., the next step is to focus on this loss in your mind. It is important to make this loss as specific as possible. Thus, as in sociotropic depression, your specific loss can be a past loss, where you recall a specific time when you were or thought you were incompetent or controlled by others. Or alternatively you can review your present life and focus on an autonomous area which isn't going too well, and evaluate this situation with a relevant irrational belief as detailed above until you conclude that you have experienced a significant loss.

Making yourself autonomously depressed: evaluate your specific loss with a specific irrational belief

Once you have focused on a loss, the next step is to evaluate it using a specific version of your general irrational belief. Thus, let's suppose that you have identified a recent situation where you have been taken off a project at work by your boss. Using your general irrational belief – 'I must be able to determine my fate and it's terrible if I can't' – you translate being taken off the project into the inference that your fate is being determined by your boss. Focusing on this specific loss, evaluate it with a specific version of your general belief, namely: 'My boss must not determine my fate and it's terrible if he does.'

Making yourself autonomously depressed: act depressed

Once again, now that you feel depressed about this specific loss, it is important that you maintain and even deepen that depression by acting in ways that are consistent with your depressed mood. Returning to our example, experiment with the following to see which deepens your depression:

- Don't see your boss to present a case for remaining on the project.
- Give up work on other work projects you are involved in.

- Play depressing music, or read depressing novels or poetry (particularly those that deal with others controlling your fate).
- Talk to people at work who are in control of their fate and compare your situation with theirs.

Making yourself autonomously depressed: think depressed

As I said earlier, depression-related irrational beliefs influence your subsequent thinking in that it becomes highly distorted in negative ways. These thinking errors will help you to deepen your depression. Let me show you what type of thinking *stems from* the following specific depression-related autonomy irrational belief: 'My boss must not determine my fate and it's terrible if he does':

- **Black and white thinking** (taking an event and putting it into one of two black and white categories): 'I am either in control of my mate or being controlled by another person. Since my boss has taken me off the project, he is completely in control of my destiny.'
- **Overgeneralization** (taking an event and generalizing it to all other similar situations and relevant categories): 'Since my boss is in control of my destiny in this situation he is in control of my destiny in all work-related situations.'
- **Always–never thinking** (taking an event and thinking that it will be like this for ever or it will never change): 'I'll never be in charge of my fate again. I'll always be under the control of this boss and other bosses.'
- **Exaggeration** (using an event as a springboard to make extreme and exaggerated statements about it and matters relating to it): 'My life is ruined if I don't have complete control of my fate.'
- **Negative prediction** (taking an event and making negative predictions about it and matters relating to it): 'Wherever I work, my destiny will not be my own.'
- **Ignoring the positive** (making one event colour everything in your life so that you ignore the positive): here you edit out the many instances where you have control of aspects of your work. Your depression-related irrational belief leads you to do this.
- **Helplessness** (editing out your personal resourcefulness to change matters on a broad scale): 'I can't do anything to change the fact that others will be in charge of my fate. Something could be done about it, but I don't have the resources to do it.'

29

- **Hopelessness** (seeing no hope for the future): 'No matter what happens, others will be in charge of my fate. I have the resources to change matters, but they can't be changed.'

Once again, if you find yourself correcting these errors go back and rehearse your original specific irrational belief. Doing so will then help you to return to making your thinking errors and will help you to sustain your feelings of depression.

Finally, don't forget that a particularly potent combination of thinking errors in the deepening of depression is helplessness and hopelessness. In this context, show yourself that you don't have the resources to determine your own fate (helplessness) and that even if you did it wouldn't change anything (hopelessness).

Making yourself autonomously depressed: evaluate your subsequent negative thinking with irrational beliefs, and keep doing this until you feel hopeless

The next step in deepening your depression is to focus on the content of your thinking error and evaluate this with another specific irrational belief. For example, imagine that you have created the following thinking error and are now focusing on it: 'Wherever I work my destiny will not be my own.' Now evaluate this with the following irrational belief: 'Wherever I work my destiny must be my own and if it's not it is completely intolerable.'

What will in all probability happen is that your subsequent thinking will be even more negative and distorted (e.g. 'I won't be able to control my destiny in life. Life will always be bleak and hopeless'). Once again you will notice at this point that you are feeling hopeless about the future, which is exactly what is needed if you are going to be really adept at making yourself depressed. But if you need extra help, implement some or all of the strategies I listed at the beginning of this chapter under the section entitled 'Preparing the ground for depression'. This will keep you in your hopeless frame of mind.

Making yourself autonomously depressed: use metaphors and images

I mentioned earlier when discussing sociotropic depression that using metaphors and images depicting this form of depression is often useful in giving you a clear focus for your depression. Such a clear focus will, of course, help you to deepen your depression because you have a vivid reminder of how miserable your life is. Let me help you do the same for autonomous depression. Here are a few suggestions that depict the hopelessness of this type of depression.

- 'My life is full of failure and defeat.'
- 'I see others succeeding and reaching their goals, but I have no chance of doing likewise. It's like walking through very thick treacle.'
- 'I am a puppet and other people are pulling my strings.'
- 'I see myself in a nightmare where I can't look after myself, so others have to look after me.'

Once again, if you practise rehearsing such metaphors and images you will maintain and even deepen your sense of hopelessness.

How to deepen your depression even further: make sociotropic and autonomous depression interact

You now know how to make yourself both sociotropically and autonomously depressed. You can use this knowledge to deepen your depression by making these two different types interact. While it is likely that you may veer more naturally to one type than the other, learning to be proficient at both and particularly at how to trigger one naturally from the other is a good skill to learn, particularly if you want to become a black belt at depression.

How to make yourself autonomously depressed after you have made yourself sociotropically depressed

So, let me start with sociotropic depression and show you how you can use this type of depression to make yourself autonomously depressed as well. Let's assume that you think your boss is annoyed with you, and that you have made yourself sociotropically depressed about this because you have evaluated his presumed annoyance with the following irrational belief: 'My boss must not be annoyed with me and if he is then this proves that I am unlikeable.' As I showed you earlier in this chapter (see pp. 24–5), holding a sociotropic depression-related irrational belief leads you to think in ways that are negative and distorted in nature. Now, if you look at the thinking errors I listed in that section, you will see that the *content* of the

31

thinking errors that stem from sociotropic depression-related irrational beliefs is sociotropic in nature. Thus in this example, where your boss, in your mind, demonstrates annoyance at you and you believe that he must not be annoyed at you and you are unlikeable if he does, you are likely to have thoughts such as 'If my boss is annoyed at me, others will be too', which are sociotropic in content.

In order to make yourself depressed autonomously after you have made yourself depressed sociotropically, you first need to make your thinking that stems from your sociotropic depression-related irrational belief autonomous in nature. Thus, if you believe that your boss must not be annoyed with you and you are unlikeable if he does, then when he does demonstrate annoyance at you, show yourself in your subsequent thinking that your boss will not give you the promotion that he promised, which is an autonomous-related thought.

Then focus on this distorted autonomous thought, treat it as if it were true and evaluate it with an irrational belief such as: 'I must advance in my career and it's terrible if I don't.' Doing this will have the following effects:

- You will feel autonomously depressed (don't forget that you already feel sociotropically depressed).
- Subsequently, you will tend to think such distorted autonomous-related thoughts as: 'There's no point in me working hard since I will never advance in my career.'
- You will tend to give up working hard at work, thereby increasing the chances of not getting promoted.

How to make yourself sociotropically depressed after you have made yourself autonomously depressed

Now let me show you how you can make yourself sociotropically depressed after you have made yourself autonomously depressed. Let's assume that you think that you are struggling at work, and that you have made yourself autonomously depressed about this because you have evaluated your struggling irrational belief: 'I must always do well at work and if I don't then I am a failure.' Again, holding an autonomous depression-related irrational belief leads you to think in ways that are negative and distorted in nature, and the content of such thinking will be largely autonomous. In the example that I am using here, you consider that you are struggling at work and you believe that you must always do well and that you are a failure if you don't: thus, you are likely to have thoughts such as 'Because I am struggling at work, I'll lose my job,' which are autonomous in content.

In order to make yourself depressed sociotropically after you have made yourself depressed autonomously, you first need to make your thinking that stems from your autonomous depression-related irrational belief sociotropic in nature. Thus, if you believe that you must always do well at work and you are a failure if you don't, then when you focus on struggling at work, show yourself in your subsequent thinking that your work colleagues will shun you once they see that you are struggling – a sociotropic-related thought.

Then focus on this distorted sociotropic thought, treat it as if it were true and evaluate it with an irrational belief such as: 'I must have good relations with my work colleagues and if I don't then I am unlikeable.' Doing so will have the following effects:

- You will feel sociotropically depressed (don't forget that you already feel autonomously depressed).
- Subsequently, you will tend to think such distorted sociotropic-related thoughts as: 'If my work colleagues don't want to know me, nobody will want to know me.'
- You will tend to withdraw socially, thereby increasing the chances of losing contact with people and reinforcing the thought that nobody wants to know you.

How to depress yourself by pitying yourself and others

As you are working towards making yourself depressed and I'm doing my best to help you to do this to a very high level of competence, I would not be doing my job if I did not teach you how to feel sorry for yourself and for others, a key component in some depressions.

How to make yourself depressed by feeling sorry for yourself

In order to feel sorry for *yourself* (rather than for the bad position that you are in), I suggest that you take the following steps:

1 Focus on an aspect of your life where you consider you have been treated badly or where you have failed to achieve something you have worked very hard for. It is important that you select an aspect of your life where you clearly think that you did not deserve the bad treatment and that you deserved to achieve what you were striving for. To really get your self-pity juices going, it is best if you select aspects where others who in your view deserved bad treatment actually received good treatment, and where others, who in your view had not worked as hard as you, achieved what you wanted to achieve.

2 Evaluate these situations (which may be accurate, but don't have to be) with the following irrational belief:

- 'I must not be treated badly when I don't deserve to be (and when others who do deserve to be treated badly aren't) and when this occurs it's terrible and the world is a rotten place for allowing this to happen to a poor undeserving person like me.'
- 'When I work hard for something I must get what I think I deserve (particularly when others who don't deserve it get what I should have got) and when I don't it's terrible and the world is a rotten place for allowing this to happen to a poor undeserving person like me.'

3 Use these irrational beliefs to influence your subsequent thinking. As I have shown several times in this book, once you evaluate a threat to or a loss from your personal domain with an irrational belief, then this belief influences your subsequent thinking in highly distorted negative ways.

Thus, when you think that you have undeservedly been treated badly and you hold an irrational belief about this, as shown the first point in (2) above, you will tend to:

- think about all the other occasions where you have been treated badly when you haven't merited such treatment;
- focus on all the unfairnesses that you have suffered and edit out all the unfairnesses that have been in your favour (which you probably think of as fairnesses).

Also, when you have worked hard for something and haven't been awarded it while others less deserving of the award have received it, and you hold an irrational belief about this, as detailed in the second point in (2) above, then you will tend to:

- think about all the other occasions when your hard work failed to be rewarded and edit out all the occasions when you have been rewarded for not working particularly hard;
- think about all the occasions when others have been rewarded for not working particularly hard and edit out occasions when their efforts have also not been rewarded.

You can then evaluate these distorted thoughts with irrational beliefs to deepen your 'poor me' depression even further.

4 Seek out people who are likely to share your 'unhealthy' views about unfairness and tell them about your hard luck story. In all probability they will respond with statements containing or implying irrational beliefs (e.g. 'Oh my God, poor you. How terrible for you'). You will probably react to such statements positively because they validate your way of looking at things, so that's good. What is even better is that such statements also help you to strengthen your conviction in self-pity-related irrational beliefs.

How to make yourself depressed by feeling sorry for others

In order to feel sorry for others (rather than for their plight, which is the healthy position and therefore should be avoided at all costs), I suggest that you take the following steps:

1 Focus on an aspect of life where you consider that other people are being treated very badly through no fault of their own. To really get your other-pity juices going, it is best if you select a situation where the other people involved are clearly helpless victims (cruelty or abusive behaviour towards a child is a particularly good scenario to focus on).

2 Evaluate these situations (which may be accurate, but don't have to be) with the following irrational belief:

- 'The world must not allow such bad treatment to happen and because it does the world is a rotten place. It is the end of the world for such treatment to be meted out to the poor person (or people).'

3 Use this irrational belief to influence your subsequent thinking. Thus, when you think that others have been treated badly through

no fault of their own and you hold an irrational belief about this (as shown above), you will tend to:

- focus on all the unfairnesses and bad treatment that innocent 'victims' have had to endure, and edit out all the fairnesses that yet others have benefited from. In short, you focus on man's inhumanity to man and edit out man's humanity to man. It will be helpful here for you to keep a scrapbook of such inhumane treatment and perhaps record news stories and documentaries of this ilk;
- think that the world is getting worse in this respect and that there is no hope for humankind.

You can then evaluate these distorted thoughts with irrational beliefs to deepen your other-pity depression even further.

4 Once again, seek out people who are likely to share your 'unhealthy' views about the fact that people can treat others abominably. This should help to strengthen your conviction in your unhealthy beliefs.

5 Whatever you do, don't do anything practical that might help these innocent 'victims'. Just be passive and complain externally and internally about how horrible the world is.

How to depress yourself about your depression

One of the great talents you have as a human being is to disturb yourself about your disturbances. As far as we know, no other organism has this ability, so on the basis that it is no use having a talent unless you use it, I am going to show you how to exploit this talent to the full by teaching you how you can depress yourself about having depression.

There are many ways that you can depress yourself about your depression, and in this part of this chapter I will cover the main ways. Once you get the hang of how to do this, you can become creative and depress yourself about your depression in unique ways.

How to depress yourself about the physical aspects of depression

Depression can be physically painful. You may, for example, have difficulty sleeping, you may lose your appetite and you may even have physical aches and pains. You can further depress yourself about the physical aspects of your depression by doing the following:

- Focus on the physical aspects of your depression.
- Practise reviewing the following irrational belief: 'I must not feel so bad and I can't bear doing so.'
- Indulge yourself in the behavioural and thinking consequences of this belief:
  Behavioural consequence: remain inert and don't do anything remotely enjoyable. This should have the desired effect of helping you focus even more on the increased physical pain of your deepening depression.
  Thinking consequence: 'I'll never get over this pain. It is just unremitting.'

Depreciate yourself about the fact that you have depressed yourself

You have a number of options here, and I will group them together. Choose the best way for you to depreciate yourself for having depression.

1 Focus on what being depressed means for you, e.g. a weakness, a failing, an evidence of having an unlovable trait.
2 Practise reviewing one of the following irrational beliefs and indulge yourself in the illustrative behavioural and thinking consequences of this belief:

- 'I must not be weak (by being depressed) and the fact that I have such a weakness means that I am a weak person.'
  Behavioural consequence: hide away from people.
  Thinking consequence: think of past instances when you have been weak; think that you will always be weak.
- 'Being depressed means that I am failing. I must not fail in this respect and the fact that I have failed proves that I am a failure.'
  Behavioural consequence: don't try anything in case you fail.
  Thinking consequence: focus on past failures, and think that you will always fail.
- 'Being depressed demonstrates that I have an unlovable trait which I must not have. Because I have it, this proves that I am an unlovable person.'
  Behavioural consequence: stay away from loved ones when depressed; try to put on a brave face when with loved ones.

Thinking consequence: think that you are bound to be rejected by anyone that you care for if they see that you are depressed.

Develop and rehearse a view of the world founded on depression-based irrational beliefs

I mentioned in the previous chapter that people develop world views that render them vulnerable to particular unhealthy negative emotions. This is certainly the case with depression. The world views that render you vulnerable to depression do so primarily because they make it very easy for you to make unhealthy anger-related inferences. Then, as I have shown you earlier in this chapter, you make yourself depressed about these inferences with the appropriate irrational beliefs. Here is an illustrative list of world views for you to develop and rehearse, together with the inferences that they spawn.

World view: Life is meaningless

Inference: No matter what I do, ultimately it is meaningless.

World view: People will ultimately reject me

Inference: If people get to know the real me they will reject me.

World view: The world is made up of strong and weak people

Inference: If I am not strong and independent, I am weak and dependent.

If you have rigorously applied the principles described in this chapter, you should now be quite adept at making yourself depressed. If not, give this book to someone who could benefit from it, because you obviously can't!

3

How to Make Yourself Feel Ashamed

Shame and guilt are often linked together in people's minds and are often seen as similar emotions. While there are certain similarities to these two emotions, they also have important differences and as such they warrant a separate chapter each. Consequently, I will teach you how to make yourself feel ashamed in this chapter and how to make yourself feel guilty in the next.

How to make yourself feel ashamed: general steps

In order to make yourself feel ashamed and stay ashamed you have to take the following steps:

1 Make an inference about what you are focusing on.
2 Appraise that inference using shame-based irrational beliefs.
3 Think in ways that are consistent with the above irrational beliefs.
4 Act in ways that are consistent with these irrational beliefs.
5 Rehearse a general version of your specific shame-based irrational beliefs so that you can become skilled at making shame-based inferences about what is generally going on in your life.
6 Develop and rehearse a shame-based world view.

So let me deal with these issues one at a time.

Make shame-related inferences

In order to feel ashamed, you need to make one or more inferences about what is going on in your life. It is important to note that these inferences don't have to reflect accurately what happened. The important point is that you have to believe that they are true. Here is a list of common shame-related inferences:

'I've fallen short of my ideal'
Focus on some aspect of your life where you consider that you have fallen short of your ideal, particularly in relation to some social code. To prime the shame pump, as it were, focus particularly on some

experience where you fell very short of your ideal and in a setting where others were physically present. If others weren't physically present then imagine that they were or that they have discovered what you did (or didn't do).

Here are some suggestions of what you can focus on under this heading to begin the shame experience:

- *Focus on your behaviour*: this could concern what you did or what you failed to do. Here are some examples to help you.
  1 Identify something that you did that constitutes a weakness in your eyes (e.g. crying in public, acting foolishly in public).
  2 Identify an incident where you broke a social code (e.g. you spoke about a taboo topic in front of a group of people).
  3 Identify an incident where you failed to live up to your social code (e.g. you consider it to be important to treat people politely, but you acted rudely to a waiter).
- *Focus on your thoughts and images*: here are some examples of thoughts and images which you might feel ashamed about:
  1 Think of harming your child.
  2 Picture yourself having sex with a member of your own sex when you are not gay.
  3 Think blasphemous thoughts.
- *Focus on your emotions and their expression*: some examples are:
  1 Feel unhealthily angry towards significant others.
  2 Show your anger in a 'nasty' way.
  3 Feel maliciously envious towards a friend for being pregnant.
  4 Demonstrate your unhealthy jealousy in public.
  If you have trouble making yourself unhealthily angry, envious or jealous, read the appropriate chapter in this book.
- *Focus on your body*: here, you might feel ashamed of some aspect of your body that you consider to be particularly unattractive. For example:
  1 Focus on the size of your nose if you think it is too big.
  2 Focus on the size of your buttocks and/or thighs if you think they are too big.
  3 Focus on the size of your penis if you think it is too small.
  3 Focus on the size of your breasts if you think they are too large or too small.

'I've let down my reference group'

A reference group is a group with whom you closely identify. You probably have a number of reference groups in your life – for example, your family, your friendship group, your religious group and your cultural group. Each of these groups has 'let-down' rules – if you break these behavioural rules, members of that group would consider that you have let them down. While it is better if the reference group you have in mind actually would 'feel' let down by you, this is not a necessary condition.

Now, follow these steps:

1 Identify a particular reference group and one of their 'let-down' rules.
2 Break the rule.
3 Think that the group 'feels' let down by you.

Here are some examples of how you can let down your reference group:

- marrying out of your religion;
- getting caught stealing;
- displaying emotion in public.

'I've been let down by a member of my reference group'

Another good way to feel ashamed involves you identifying an incident where a member of your reference group broke one of the group's 'let-down' rules and then thinking that the person has let you and the group down. Good examples are the same as the above, namely where the other has:

- married out of your religion;
- been caught stealing;
- displayed emotion in public.

'Others are judging me negatively'

It is difficult to feel ashamed without making the inference that another person – or, more frequently, a group of people – is judging you negatively. Again, whether they are or not is not as important as whether you think they are. Also, while it is useful to have the judging group present in order to get those shame juices really flowing, their physical presence isn't necessary. You can feel ashamed while imagining this group judging you negatively.

What type of judgements do you think others make of you when you feel ashamed? Here you have a choice, so pick the one that best fits the episode in which you are attempting to make yourself feel ashamed:

- Others communicate their displeasure at you directly.
- Others communicate their disgust at you directly.
- Others turn away from you in disgust.
- Others demonstrate that they look down on you.
- Others ignore you.

If you find it difficult to find a group of people likely to communicate one or more of the above reactions to you, practise being on the receiving end of such reactions in your imagination. The more vividly you can imagine these negative reactions towards you, the better.

Hold and rehearse irrational beliefs about your inference

If there is a main point that I want to stress in this book it is that you will find it difficult to disturb yourself unless you hold a set of irrational beliefs about the inferences that you make. In this context, you will not feel ashamed about falling short of your ideal, letting down your reference group, being let down by a member of your reference group, and/or others evaluating you negatively without holding irrational beliefs about these inferences.

So let me teach you how to feel ashamed by showing you which irrational beliefs to develop and rehearse about the above inferences. In doing this, it is important that you hold a rigid demand and a self-depreciation belief about your inferences that I will discuss and demonstrate below. In doing so I will outline the general irrational belief and illustrate it with a specific example.

How to make yourself ashamed about falling short of your ideal

In general, in order to feel ashamed about falling short of your ideal you need to hold a rigid demand about such a falling short (e.g. 'I must not fall short of my ideal') and a self-depreciation about your shortfall (e.g. '. . . and because I have fallen short I am an inadequate person'). For example, let's assume that your ideal is to handle matters without showing anger, and one day at work you lose your temper in front of your work colleagues. In order to make yourself feel ashamed about your shortfall, hold and practise the following shame-based irrational belief: 'I must not lose my temper in public and because I did I am an inadequate person.'

How to make yourself ashamed about letting down your reference group

In general, to feel ashamed about letting down your reference group you again need to hold a rigid demand about such a letting down (e.g. 'I must not let my reference group down') and a consequent self-depreciation belief (e.g. '. . . and because I have let them down, I am a shameful person'). For example, let's assume that you belong to a gang whose code of honour is always to support one another no matter what, and let's suppose further that you break that code by failing to support another member, thus letting down the gang. In order to make yourself feel ashamed about your behaviour, hold and practise the following shame-based irrational belief: 'I absolutely should not have betrayed my fellow gang member and because I did I am a shameful person.'

How to make yourself feel ashamed about being let down by a member of your reference group

In general, in order to feel ashamed about being let down by your reference group you need to hold a rigid demand about such a let-down (e.g. 'A member of my reference group must not let me and the group down') and a self-depreciation belief about this situation (e.g. '. . . and because they have let us down, it proves that we are inadequate'). For example, let's assume that your reference group holds dear not crying in public, and that one day a member of your reference group (Fred) does cry in front of others: you view this as that person letting you and your reference group down. In order to make yourself feel ashamed about this let-down, hold and practise the following shame-based irrational belief: 'Fred absolutely should not have broken down in tears in front of other people, and because he did it proves that we are all (in our reference group) inadequate, weak, spineless individuals.'

How to make yourself feel ashamed when others judge you negatively in a shame-related context, or you think that they do

In general, to feel ashamed when others judge you negatively in a shame-related context (and again, what is important here is that you think that they are judging you, rather than the facts of the situation), you once again need to hold a rigid demand about such a negative judgement (e.g. 'Others must not judge me negatively') and a self-depreciation belief concerning this judgement (e.g. '. . . and because they have judged me negatively, it proves that I am inadequate'). For example, let's assume that you have spoken up in a social context and mentioned something that was a taboo in that group. Let's further assume that you think that those present have turned away from you in disgust. In order to feel ashamed about this negative judgement, hold and practise the following shame-based irrational belief: 'This group absolutely should not have turned away from me in disgust and because they did it proves that I am inadequate.'

Develop competence at making shame-based negative self-judgements

I have made it clear in this section that the essence of making yourself feel ashamed is to hold and practice shame-based irrational beliefs. Moreover, I have stressed that these irrational beliefs have two major components: a rigid demand and a self-depreciation belief. Now, a rigid demand is straightforward. It is absolute and comes in the form of a must, absolute should, have to, got to, among others. Self-depreciation beliefs in shame are more varied, and I want to outline the major shame-based negative self-judgements so that you can use the most appropriate one for you. It is worth learning them all, however, as a major cornerstone for making yourself feel ashamed in as many contexts as possible. Before I list these self-depreciation beliefs, I just want to remind you that a self-depreciation belief involves you making a global negative judgement about your entire self. You are not rating a part of yourself, you are rating the whole of you.

'I am defective'

People who feel ashamed often say: 'There is something wrong with me.' They don't mean that they are a fallible human being who may be defective in some respect. Rather, they mean that they are defective as a whole. In expressing this view, one of my clients said: 'If I was a car, the garage would say that I was beyond repair and should be scrapped.' So, in order to make yourself ashamed, focus on an aspect of yourself that is negative and could do with improvement, and then overgeneralize from this to the whole of you. In essence, learn to say and believe the following: 'Because this part of me is defective then I am defective.' As you will see, this process of overgeneralizing from a part of you to the whole of you is common to all shame-based negative self-judgements, so learn this skill well.

'I am insignificant'

Sometimes when people feel ashamed they say that they 'feel small'. Behind this 'feeling' is the self-depreciation belief 'I am insignificant', and if you hold this belief it is often in response to a situation where you have inferred, rightly or wrongly, that another person has belittled you in public. This shows that if you want to feel ashamed then it is very useful to judge yourself in the same way as you think the other person has judged you, especially, of course, when this judgement is negative. A handy phrase to remember in this context is: 'I am the person I think you say I am.'

'I am not good enough'

As I have already stated, people often feel ashamed when they fall short of their ideal. As I noted when discussing the 'I am defective' shame-based self-depreciation belief, people experiencing shame often make the part–whole error. This is also true when the content of the self-depreciation belief is 'I am not good enough'. Here, begin by noting that you have failed to measure up to your ideal in some way. In this *part* of your life we may say that you are not good enough *in this respect*. Then overgeneralize from this aspect to your entire self. For example: 'Because I am not good enough at public speaking, I am not good enough as a person.'

'I am weak/pathetic'

If you listen to the self-evaluations of people who experience much shame in their lives, you will often hear them refer to themselves as being weak or pathetic. Thus, one of the ideals that such people demand they must achieve is some sort of 'strength', either physical or mental. The latter, particularly, is prominent in shame. So if you want to feel ashamed in this area, focus on some aspect of your life where you are not as strong as you absolutely should be. Then globally rate yourself as weak or pathetic. For example, imagine that you consider it weak to cry in public and that you do, in fact, do this in front of other people. In order to make yourself feel ashamed about this weak display, hold and practise the following irrational belief: 'I must not cry in public and because I did I am a pathetic weak person.'

'I am disgusting'

The final way to make yourself feel ashamed is to view yourself as a disgusting person. A good focus for your self-disgust is your body. Imagine that you have fat thighs. Now, there are two ways of making yourself feel ashamed about the way that you look in this respect. First, make a rigid demand about your thighs – 'My thighs absolutely should not be fat' – and then rate yourself as disgusting: 'Because my thighs look disgusting I am disgusting.' You can repeat this process for any aspect of your body that you particularly dislike.

Make yourself feel ashamed by evaluating yourself according to what happened to you

One good way of making yourself feel ashamed is by evaluating yourself according to what happened to you. Thus, if another person has ridiculed you in public, tell yourself that this ridicule proves that you are a stupid, shameful person.

How to experience unconditional shame

So far, I have discussed how to make yourself conditionally ashamed, which means that you feel ashamed when the conditions are right – when you think that you have fallen short of your ideal, let down your reference group, been let down by a member of your reference group, and/or been evaluated negatively by others. Some people, however, think they are insignificant, defective or disgusting, etc., because they are alive or because of who they are. In other words, their shame is unconditional. Consequently, it is unremitting and ever-present. If you want to experience unconditional shame, try to convince yourself that you are insignificant, defective or disgusting, etc., because you are alive or because you are who you are. You might not believe it, but what have you got to lose?

Think in ways that are consistent with your shame-based irrational beliefs

When you hold a shame-based irrational belief about thinking that you have fallen very short of your ideal, you have let down your reference group, you have been let down by a member of your reference group, and/or others are judging you negatively, this belief will influence the way that you subsequently think. If you practise these forms of thinking (which I will presently list) then you will refine your ability to make yourself experience shame. So when you begin to experience shame because of the shame-based irrational beliefs you hold, think in some of the following ways that are characterized by exaggeration, overestimation of negative consequences and failure to appreciate that there may be a variety of responses to your behaviour. To exemplify such thinking, let's assume that you have made yourself feel ashamed about saying something stupid in front of a group of people.

Overestimate the 'shamefulness' of your behaviour

Think that what you said was very stupid (rather than moderately or mildly stupid).

Overestimate the extent to which others will notice your 'shameful' behaviour

Think that everyone present took notice of what you said.

Overestimate the likelihood that others will regard your behaviour as 'shameful'

Think that it is highly likely that everyone present thought that what you said was stupid.

Overestimate the extent to which others will regard your behaviour as 'shameful'

Think that they regarded your behaviour as very stupid (rather than moderately or mildly stupid).

Overestimate the length of time that others will remember your 'shameful' behaviour

Think that those present will remember what you said for a very long time.

Overestimate the likelihood that others will regard you as 'shameful'

Think that it is highly likely that those present thought that you were stupid (rather than that just your behaviour was stupid).

Overestimate the extent to which others will regard you as 'shameful'

Think that those present thought that you were very stupid (rather than mildly or moderately stupid).

Overestimate the length of time that others will regard you as 'shameful'

Think that those present will consider you stupid for a very long time.

Overestimate the likelihood that those observing will tell others about you

Think that it is highly likely that those present will tell others about what you said.

Exaggerate what those observing will tell others about you

Think that those present will tell others what a very stupid person you are.

Exaggerate the extent to which others will ridicule you

Think that those present will ridicule you very badly.

Exaggerate the extent to which others will exclude you

Think that those present will exclude you and not want anything to do with you in the future.

Act in ways that are consistent with your shame-based irrational beliefs

If you have followed and implemented what I have said so far, you should be able to make yourself feel ashamed. The next step is to maintain and even deepen that sense of shame by acting in ways that are consistent with your shame-based irrational beliefs.

You will note that many of these behaviours are both an expression of shame and an attempt by you to avoid the pain of these feelings. The main point to note is that these behaviours stem from your shame-based irrational beliefs, and when you engage in them they help to strengthen your conviction in these beliefs. As such, engaging in shame-based behaviours renders you more vulnerable to experiencing shame, which after all is your objective.

Physically withdraw from others

When you feel ashamed, you will experience a strong tendency to physically withdraw from the people who you think have witnessed your 'shameful' behaviour and are evaluating you negatively for it. When you give in to this tendency and actually withdraw from these people, you will immediately experience a sense of relief, but don't worry – this will be short-lived, and withdrawing this way will help you to experience shame in the future because you have strengthened your shame-based irrational beliefs. By physically withdrawing from others after revealing a weakness to them, for example, you are in effect saying: 'If I remain in the presence of these people after acting weakly in front of them, I will see them look down on me, and this will mean that I am a weak person for acting weakly which I absolutely should not have done. Therefore I will leave.'

Look away from others

When you feel shame in the presence of others, you will tend to look down and away from their gaze. Don't resist this tendency, since it will help you to strengthen your shame-based irrational belief. Use it when you are not able to physically withdraw from the social situation in which you find yourself, since it is a form of psychological withdrawal. It strengthens your shame-based irrational belief in a similar way that physically withdrawing from others does. By looking away from others after revealing a weakness to them, for example, you are in effect saying: 'If I look at these people after acting weakly in front of them, I will see them look down on me, and this will mean that I am a weak person for acting weakly which I absolutely should not have done. Therefore I will avoid their gaze.'

Isolate yourself from others

Once you feel ashamed, and perhaps after you have physically withdrawn from the shame-related situation, a good way to perpetuate your shame-based irrational belief is by isolating yourself from others. By doing so you are in effect saying: 'Because I am a disgusting person for revealing my fat thighs in public, I'll avoid other people in case they see them.'

Deny responsibility for your actions

When you have made yourself feel ashamed, you will be tempted to get rid of these feelings of shame by denying responsibility for your actions. Give in to your temptation, because in doing so you will perpetuate your shame-based irrational beliefs and make it more likely that you will feel shame in the future. Let me show you how to do this. Imagine that you have insulted your boss's husband at the works Christmas party. You begin to feel ashamed because you believe that you have shown yourself to be stupid. To get rid of these feelings, quickly deny responsibility for your actions by blaming them on the medication that you claim to be taking (but in reality are not). In doing so, you will be strengthening your shame-creating irrational beliefs.

Conceal verbally and physically

Shame and concealment often go together. You can hide when you feel ashamed and you can hide in order to prevent yourself from feeling ashamed. Either way, when you act in a concealing manner you reinforce your shame-based irrational beliefs.

When you use verbal concealment, decide to say very little about yourself to others. Be quite superficial in your conversations and certainly do not say anything that might be taken as controversial by those present. The reason you conceal is to avoid feeling ashamed. It is as if you are saying to yourself: 'I will not reveal anything that could be construed as controversial about myself, because if I do others may look down on me and I must not be disapproved of by others. If this happens it proves that I am inadequate.'

When concealment is physical, hide aspects of your body from others. Do this because you feel ashamed of yourself for having such aspects. Again, your concealment is underpinned by a shame-creating irrational belief: 'Others must not see how fat my thighs are and if they do they will think that I am disgusting and they would be right. I am disgusting for having fat thighs. Therefore, I will hide them from public view.'

Overcompensate for your feelings of shame

Another way to perpetuate your shame-creating irrational belief, and thus make it more likely that you will feel shame, is to act in a way that overcompensates for your shame. Thus, if you feel ashamed of being of small and weak stature, overcompensate for this by showing everyone how physically strong you are.

In order to overcompensate for your feelings of shame, therefore, it is important for you to do the very opposite of what you feel ashamed about.

Develop and rehearse general shame-based irrational beliefs

General shame-based irrational beliefs are irrational beliefs that you hold in many theme-related situations which enable you to experience shame in these situations. If you develop and rehearse such beliefs, you will enable yourself to experience shame in many different situations. You will do this mainly because you will become skilled at inferring, for example, that you have fallen short of your ideal and that other people will evaluate you negatively for this, even when there is scant supporting evidence for the latter.

Let me show you how this works. First, develop general shame-based irrational beliefs such as: 'I must always live up to my ideals and if I don't then I am inadequate' and 'Other people must not disapprove of me and if they do it proves that I am inadequate.' Now rehearse these beliefs until you firmly believe them and you bring them to relevant situations where it is possible that you will not live up to your ideal and that others will disapprove of you. Then, because you cannot convince yourself that you will live up to your ideal and that you will not be disapproved of, think that you have fallen short of your ideal (in a big way) and that people will disapprove of you for this. Having created these shame-based inferences, evaluate them using specific versions of these general shame-based irrational beliefs, and thereby make yourself feel ashamed in the specific situation.

Let me give you a concrete example of how to do this. Develop the following two general shame-based irrational beliefs: 'I must never lose my temper in public and if I do I am a weak person' and 'Others must approve of me and if they don't I am inadequate.' Imagine taking these two beliefs to a specific situation, where a waiter in a restaurant brought you the wrong dish and you snapped at him very briefly. These two general shame-based irrational beliefs will lead you to make the following inferences about this event: 'I lost my temper with the waiter' (because of your first general shame-based irrational belief, you inferred that snapping briefly at the waiter was tantamount to losing your temper with him) and 'Others witnessing this disapproved of me for losing my temper with the waiter' (because of your second general shame-based irrational belief, you inferred that because those present would not approve of you for this incident they would disapprove of you for it; your belief does not permit you to consider that they might think you were justified in your behaviour, or that they did not take any notice, or that they might briefly disapprove of your behaviour but still basically approve of you).

Once you have created your inferences, make yourself feel ashamed about them by evaluating them with specific versions of your irrational beliefs, thus: 'I lost my temper with the waiter and incurred the disapproval of those present. I absolutely should not have done either of these things and because I did I am a weak, inadequate person.' Then, think and act in ways that are consistent with your shame and that will strengthen your conviction in shame-based irrational beliefs, and you will put the icing on your shame cake.

Develop and rehearse a view of the world founded on shame-based irrational beliefs

People develop ideas about the world as it relates to them, and some of these world views render them vulnerable to particular unhealthy negative emotions. The world views that render you vulnerable to shame do so because they make it very easy for you to make shame-related inferences. Then, as I have shown you earlier in this chapter, you make yourself feel ashamed about these inferences with the appropriate irrational beliefs. Here is an illustrative list of shame-related world views for you to develop and rehearse, together with the inferences that they spawn.

World view: There is always the danger that I will not achieve my ideal standards

Inference: I have not reached my ideal and am showing a weakness.

World view: Social situations are dangerous because other people will judge me negatively if I put a foot wrong

Inference: If I make a *faux pas*, people will judge me negatively.

World view: Social situations are dangerous because I may be exposed at any moment

Inference: If I reveal a weakness, people will judge me negatively.

I hope you can see how you can become really adept at creating shame for yourself. I will now move on to teach you how to become really adept at making yourself feel guilty.

4

How to Make Yourself Feel Guilty

Guilt is a particularly painful emotion and one that it is important to add to your repertoire if you are going to make yourself truly emotionally disturbed. I will first outline the general steps that you need to take to make yourself feel guilty before discussing each step in some detail.

Before I do so, a word on terminology. I make the distinction between *being* guilty and *feeling* guilty. By being guilty, I mean that you take responsibility for doing something wrong, for failing to do the right thing or for harming or hurting someone. By feeling guilty, I mean the emotion that you experience when you blame or condemn yourself for one or more of the above. Because it is based on unhealthy irrational beliefs and generally has negative consequences, guilt is a disturbed negative emotion and therefore to be cultivated. A feeling of remorse is a healthy response to doing wrong, etc., because it is based on responsibility without self-blame and generally has healthy consequences. You should therefore avoid making yourself feel remorse and concentrate on feeling guilty.

How to make yourself feel guilty: general steps

In order to make yourself feel guilty and stay feeling guilty, I suggest that you take the following steps:

1 Make an inference about what you are focusing on.
2 Appraise that inference using guilt-based irrational beliefs.
3 Think in ways that are consistent with the above irrational beliefs.
4 Act in ways that are consistent with these irrational beliefs.
5 Rehearse a general version of your specific guilt-based irrational beliefs so that you can become skilled at making guilt-based inferences about what is generally going on in your life.
6 Develop and rehearse a guilt-based world view.

Now let me deal with these issues one at a time:

Make guilt-related inferences

To feel guilty, the first step is for you to make one or more inferences about what is going on in your life. Once again, these inferences don't have to reflect accurately what happened. The important point is that you have to believe that they are true. Here is a list of common guilt-related inferences:

'I have broken my moral or ethical code'

Here are some suggestions for what you can focus on under this heading to begin the guilt experience:

- badmouthing one of your friends to another friend;
- cheating on your partner;
- making racist remarks.

'I have failed to live up to my moral or ethical code'

For example:

- failing to help someone who required assistance;
- not praying every day;
- not giving to charity.

'I have harmed or hurt the feelings of others'

For example:

- forgetting your mother's birthday, with the result that she feels hurt;
- telling your child off and making them cry;
- getting someone into trouble at work.

Hold and rehearse irrational beliefs about your guilt-related inference

Once again, I want to stress that it is not your inferences that make you feel disturbed; rather, you feel disturbed because of the irrational beliefs that you hold about the inferences you make. In this context, you will not feel guilty about breaking your moral or ethical code, not living up to your moral or ethical code, or harming someone or hurting their feelings, without holding irrational beliefs about these inferences.

So let me teach you how to feel guilty by showing you which irrational beliefs to develop and rehearse about the above inferences. Once again, in doing this it is important that you hold a rigid demand and a self-depreciation belief about your inferences, as I will discuss and demonstrate below. In doing so, I will outline the general irrational belief and illustrate it with a specific example.

How to make yourself guilty about breaking your moral or ethical code

In general, to feel guilty about breaking your moral or ethical code, you need to hold a rigid demand about such a code violation (e.g. 'I must not break my moral or ethical code') and a self-depreciation about it (e.g. '. . . and because I have broken it, I am a bad person'). For example, let's assume that you think it is unethical for you to let your friends down. On one occasion you are faced with a choice of getting a free holiday and letting down a friend, or supporting your friend and missing out on the holiday. On an impulse you decide to go for the free holiday, which means that you are letting down your friend. In order to make yourself feel guilty about your code violation, hold and practise the following guilt-based irrational belief: 'I absolutely should not have let down my friend and because I did I am a bad person.'

How to make yourself feel guilty about not living up to your moral or ethical code

The difference between this situation and the above is that in the above you have committed a sin of commission: you have done the wrong thing. Here you have committed a sin of omission: you have failed to do the right thing. In general, to feel guilty about your failure to live up to your moral or ethical code, you must again hold a rigid demand about such a failure (e.g. 'I must live up to my moral or ethical code') and a consequent self-depreciation belief (e.g. '. . . and because I have not, I am a bad person'). For example, let's assume that you think going to the aid of someone is the right thing to do; you see someone being attacked, but you turn and walk away from the incident. From your frame of reference you have failed to live up to your ethical code.

To make yourself feel guilty about your behaviour, develop and practise the following guilt-based irrational belief: 'I absolutely should have gone to the aid of that person and because I didn't I am a bad person.'

How to make yourself feel guilty about harming or hurting the feelings of someone else

In general, to feel guilty about harming or hurting the feelings of someone else, hold a rigid demand about your role in this situation (e.g. 'I absolutely should not harm or hurt someone') and a self-depreciation about your role (e.g. '. . . and because I did I am a bad person'). For example, let's assume that you want to visit your parents over Easter and your partner wants to visit his (in this case) in a different part of the country. One way to make yourself feel guilty about this situation is to tell yourself: 'My partner is upset and I am the cause. I upset him which I must not do and this proves what a bad, selfish person I am.' Another way to practise your guilt-related irrational belief in this situation, but this time without feeling guilty, is to go along with your partner's wishes because you think that he would be upset about not seeing his parents (I call this a way of rehearsing emotional disturbance without feeling it). This is a situation where you would make yourself feel guilty because of the following guilt-producing irrational belief: 'If we did not go to see his parents I know that he would be upset, and I would be the cause of this. I must not upset my partner and I am a bad, selfish person if I do.'

Develop competence at making guilt-based negative self-judgements

As I have shown, the essence of making yourself feel ashamed is to hold and practise guilt-based irrational beliefs. Moreover, I have stressed that these irrational beliefs have two major components: a rigid demand and a self-depreciation belief. A rigid demand, as we have seen, is relatively straightforward. It is absolute and comes in the form of a must, absolute should, have to, got to, among others. Self-depreciation beliefs in guilt are a little more varied (although not as varied as in shame) and I want to outline the major guilt-based negative self-judgements so that you can use the most appropriate one for you. Learn them all, because you never know when they may come in handy. Before I list these self-depreciation beliefs, remember that a self-depreciation belief involves you making a global negative judgement about your entire self. You are not rating a part of yourself, you are rating the whole of you.

'I am bad'

The main form of self-depreciation in guilt is 'I am bad.' This is sometimes expressed as 'I am a bad person', 'I am rotten' or 'I am a rotten person.' The hallmark of this form of self-depreciation at the point when you are experiencing guilt is that your entire 'self' is morally corrupt. Most of the time you think this way after you have either broken your moral code, failed to live up to your moral code, or harmed or hurt someone's feelings, as I have discussed above. And when you do so you are making the part–whole error: evaluating your entire self on the basis of one of its parts. In simple terms, you jump from 'it's bad' to 'I'm bad'. For example:

- 'Because I stole stationery from my place of work, I am a bad person.'
- 'Because I failed to go to the help of that person being attacked, I am bad.'
- 'Because I hurt my sister's feelings by saying that I didn't like her new dress, I am a rotten person.'

This process of overgeneralizing from a part of you to the whole of you is common to virtually all guilt-based negative self-judgements, so learn this skill well.

'I am less good than I would have been if...'

There may be times when you resist condemning yourself as bad or rotten and thus won't make yourself feel guilty about sins of commission, omission and causing harm/hurt to others. Don't despair. If you can't go the whole hog and condemn yourself as bad or rotten, you can still make yourself feel guilty (although not as guilty as when you do go the whole hog) by evaluating yourself as less good than you would be if you hadn't done the wrong thing, if you had done the right thing or if you hadn't caused harm or hurt to others. For example, if you failed to live up to your moral/ethical code by failing to go the aid of another person, you can still make yourself feel guilty by believing: 'I absolutely should have helped that person and since I didn't I am less good than I would have been if I had helped him.'

'I am selfish'

One of the characteristics of people who experience chronic guilt (i.e. they feel guilty often and across different situations) is that in reality they tend to be selfless and put other people's interests before their own. When they even think of putting their own healthy interests before the interests of others they feel guilty and back down because they believe: 'I must make sure that others are catered for before I go for what I want, and if I put myself before others I am a selfish person.'

Learn this lesson well and you will either make yourself feel guilty if you put your healthy interests before the interests of others, or you will be miserable and strengthen your conviction in your guilt-based irrational beliefs if you put others before yourself. The following vignette illustrates this dynamic. Helen was a 40-year-old single woman who was the principal carer for her ageing mother, with whom she lived. Helen regularly put her mother's interests before her own, with the result that she rarely went out and had virtually no social life. However, she did have two old school friends who were very loyal to her. These friends badgered Helen incessantly to allow them to take her out to celebrate her fortieth birthday, even arranging for a professional carer to look after her mother. Eventually, albeit reluctantly, Helen agreed to go, after obsessively checking with her mother that she didn't mind. However, just before going into the posh restaurant that her friends had booked for the celebration, Helen made herself feel severely guilty and made her apologies before rushing home to her mother. Helen did this because she held the following belief: 'I must not enjoy myself when I know that my mother is not enjoying herself. Because I am putting my pleasure before my mother's feelings I am a selfish person.'

If you wish to use the self-evaluation of selfishness as a way to make yourself feel guilty, it is important that you shuttle between two positions: selflessness and selfishness. When you do so, you are basically saying that either you put other people's interests before your own or you are a selfish person. In order to become competent at this skill, it helps to develop the idea that as a person you are unimportant, and that the only way that you can gain a sense of importance is by ensuring that you help others achieve their goals or ensure that they don't get upset. Developing this attitude towards yourself results in you becoming highly susceptible to others manipulating you through guilt. Thus, Helen's mother successfully manipulated Helen by saying things like: 'Don't worry about me, dear, I'll be all right,' while giving her a pained expression. What this really meant, as Helen fully realized, was: 'I'll be upset if you go out and it will be all your fault.'

When you tell yourself that you are a selfish person, you are doing three things. First, you acknowledge that your behaviour is selfish; second, you assume that because you have acted selfishly you score high on the trait known as 'selfishness'; and third, you are using that trait description to define yourself. It is as if you are saying: 'Because I have acted selfishly, I have selfishness and I am therefore a selfish person.' If you become accomplished at this behaviour → trait → self-translation process, you can skip the middle step and learn to define your 'self' on the basis of your behaviour (behaviour → self) e.g.: 'Because I acted selfishly I am a selfish person.'

Finally, when you tell yourself that you are a selfish person, most of the time you are implying (although you do not explicitly say so) that you are a bad person or certainly less good than you would be if you scored highly on selflessness or acted selflessly. If the implication isn't enough to get your guilt juices flowing, make this explicit: 'Because I am a selfish person, I am bad.'

'I don't deserve good things to happen to me. I only deserve bad things . . .'

Another good way to make yourself feel unhealthily guilty is to consider yourself undeserving of good things but deserving of bad. This is a more subtle form of self-depreciation and thus should only be used as a last resort, i.e. when you cannot convince yourself that you are bad, rotten, selfish or less good than you would be if you hadn't done the wrong thing (for example). But it might work for you, so give it a try.

How to make yourself feel unconditional guilt

So far, I have discussed how to make yourself conditionally guilty, which means that you feel guilty when the conditions are right: i.e. when you have broken your moral code, failed to live up to your moral code, and/or harmed or hurt someone's feelings. Some people, however, think they are bad people because they are alive or because of who they are. In other words, their guilt is unconditional. Consequently, it is unremitting and ever-present. If you want to experience unconditional guilt, try to convince yourself that you are bad because you are alive or because you are who you are. You might not believe it, but what have you got to lose?

Think in ways that are consistent with your guilt-based irrational beliefs

When you hold a guilt-based irrational belief about thinking that you have broken your moral code, you have failed to do the right thing, and/or you have caused harm or hurt to others, this belief will influence the way that you subsequently think. If you practise these forms of thinking then you will develop your ability to make yourself experience guilt. So, when you begin to experience guilt, think in some of the following ways.

Exaggerate the badness of your behaviour

Once you have made yourself feel guilty about your 'sin', think about what you did in exaggerated ways. In particular, think that your actions are much worse than when you first focused on them. You will probably discover that you do this spontaneously once you have made yourself feel guilty about your 'sin', but if not you can keep the guilt juices flowing by exaggerating the badness of what you did deliberately. Thus, if you first made yourself feel guilty about hurting your parents' feelings by refusing to do their shopping for them, exaggerate this by showing yourself that your actions were despicably selfish. It goes without saying that in exaggerating the badness of your behaviour in this way, you will then evaluate this exaggeration with your guilt-inducing irrational belief, thus making yourself even more guilty, but should you not do it spontaneously you can always do it intentionally.

Exaggerate the negative consequences of your behaviour and minimize its positive consequences

Once you have made yourself feel guilty about your sin, exaggerate the negative consequences of your behaviour and minimize its positive consequences. Thus, once you have made yourself feel guilty about stealing stationery from work, think that you are bound to get caught, that when you do you will be fired, and that you will find it difficult to get another job (exaggerating the negative consequences of your behaviour). At the same time, edit out what you can productively learn from this episode: e.g. don't focus on the fact that you stole it because you thought that you needed it, and don't think that you can challenge the idea that you must have what you want (minimizing the positive consequences of your behaviour). Again, you will find that you will tend to engage in such thinking as a natural consequence of holding guilt-inducing beliefs, but if not, you can use your imagination to think of all kinds of negative consequences that will follow if you are a bad person for 'sinning', and be sure to dismiss from your mind any positive consequences of your behaviour, should you think of some.

Assume more personal responsibility for what happened and assign less responsibility to others than the situation warrants

Once you have made yourself feel guilty and you look back on your 'sin' and all the factors involved, assume far more responsibility than the situation warrants and assign far less responsibility to relevant others. In a phrase, think it is all your fault. If you practise thinking 'It was all my fault' and dismissing the responsibility that others had in the same situation, then you will help yourself to remain feeling guilty.

An excellent way to keep feelings of guilt alive is to edit out of the picture the responsibility that others have for their own feelings. You do this quite nicely when you think that you can hurt other people's feelings. Actually you can't hurt their feelings. In reality, you can treat people badly, harm them physically or materially, but you can't hurt their feelings since they have the choice of whether or not to disturb themselves about your behaviour towards them. However, please disregard this and cling to the belief that you can directly hurt their feelings. Otherwise you will be in danger of getting over your guilt feelings, which is not what you want to do.

Engage in 'if only' thinking

'If only' thinking is a very effective way of perpetuating guilt after you have begun to experience it, and therefore I suggest that you learn to develop and refine this skill. Let's suppose that in good faith you made a business decision which unfortunately did not work out, with the result that you had to sack two of your employees to ensure that your company continued trading. Imagine further that you have made yourself feel guilty by believing that you absolutely should not have acted in a way that had such bad consequences and that you are a bad person because you did. Maintain your guilt feelings by showing yourself that if only you hadn't acted in that way, then your two employees would not have had to be sacked. This reinforces the idea that you alone were responsible for sacking your employees. Of course, it may be true that if you hadn't made the decision then the two employees would not have lost their jobs. However, it could equally be true that if you hadn't made the decision then other bad things would have happened (and if you have properly followed the guidelines in this chapter you would make yourself feel guilty about this, too!). Now, it is very important that you don't think this way. Only tell yourself that this bad outcome would not have happened if you hadn't made the decision, and that a good outcome would have happened if you had made a different decision. In doing so, you get two guilts for the price of one. First, you make yourself feel guilty for taking sole responsibility for the bad outcome ('I am a bad person because I made a decision that resulted in me having to sack two of my employees. I absolutely should not have made such a bad decision') and second, you make yourself feel guilty for not making a different, more effective decision ('If only I made that other investment that I was considering at the time, then I would not have had to lay off my two employees and things would have flourished. I am a bad person for not making the right decision as I absolutely should have done.').

Judge what you did with the benefit of hindsight only

One of the things that people who do not make themselves feel unhealthily guilty do is to look back at their 'sin' from the perspective of when they took action. Thus, they are able to say: 'Yes, I now see that I broke my moral code, but I was so fixated on getting what I wanted, it did not occur to me that I was breaking my moral code. What I have learned from this situation is that I need to deal with my tendency to become fixated so that I can be more aware of the implications of my behaviour.' Now, if you want to make yourself feel guilty in the first place and to perpetuate these feelings in the second place, then this is definitely *not* the way to think. One way of avoiding this mode of thinking is only to judge your behaviour with the benefit of hindsight (e.g. 'I could have foreseen what I was going to do and therefore I absolutely should have done so' or 'I now see that it would have been better to do x rather than y, therefore I absolutely should have done y'). As you can see, hindsight thinking goes very nicely with absolute thinking and is a very powerful guilt-inducing cocktail. Here's a helpful phrase to memorize and use in such circumstances: 'Because I could have done things differently, I absolutely should have done things differently.'

Do not take into account mitigating factors or show yourself compassion

Once you have made yourself feel guilty you will tend to discount what might be called mitigating factors, i.e. genuine reasons that may help you take an understanding, compassionate view of your 'sin'. Good! After all, if you start to be compassionate you will tend to stop feeling guilty, which won't do at all. So be hard on yourself when it comes to the thinking that you engage in after you have made yourself feel guilty.

Fail to appreciate the complexity of the situation

When you do something wrong, for example, your behaviour is most accurately viewed from a complex perspective. Thus, when you let down your friend you may have faced a choice between letting down your friend and letting down your parents, and you decided to let down your friend because you thought that it was the lesser of the two evils. Such thinking will not do at all, because it is likely to erode guilt. So to maintain feelings of guilt, it is important that you look at things in black and white – thus, 'letting down my friend is just plain wrong and that's the end of it'. Then, of course, you can evaluate this inference with another guilt-inducing irrational belief to enhance your feelings of guilt.

Think that you will receive due retribution for your behaviour

When you make yourself feel guilty, one of the guilt-inducing irrational beliefs that you hold is that you are a bad person. When you think that you are a bad person this belief encourages you to think that bad things will happen to you because you think that you deserve retribution for being a bad person. So, if you wish to maintain your feelings of guilt, just think of the bad things that you deserve to happen to you because you are a bad person for having sinned.

Act in ways that are consistent with your guilt-based irrational beliefs

If you have followed and implemented what I have said so far, you should be able to make yourself feel guilty. The next step is to maintain and even deepen that sense of guilt by acting in ways that are consistent with your guilt-based irrational beliefs. Once again, you will note that many of these behaviours are both an expression of guilt and an attempt by you to avoid the pain of these feelings. The main point to note is that these behaviours stem from your guilt-based irrational beliefs, and when you engage in them they help to strengthen your conviction in these beliefs. Engaging in guilt-based behaviours renders you more vulnerable to experiencing guilt, which, of course, is your goal.

Confess regardless of the consequences

Some say that confession is good for the soul, and this may be the case if you think carefully about the consequences of your confession and judge that it will do you more good than harm. However, this position is too healthy for our present purposes. Rather, if you wish to deepen your guilt, confess your 'sin' to the people involved regardless of the consequences. In doing so, you will be strengthening your guilt-based irrational belief: 'I am a bad person and I must unburden myself to become good again.' Of course, confession (outside a religious context) doesn't lead you to become good again, so that won't work, and there is a very good chance that the consequences of your confession will be harmful to you and the other(s) involved. This latter point is very useful, since you can give yourself a double whammy of guilt: 'I am a bad person for doing what I did in the first place and a bad person for upsetting the other(s) by confessing my sin in the second place.' So, thoughtless confession will get you further down the guilt road, which, of course, is where you want to travel.

Beg for forgiveness

Another way to strengthen your guilt-based irrational beliefs is to beg the person you have wronged, harmed or hurt for forgiveness. In order to strengthen your guilt-inducing philosophy, don't just *ask* to be forgiven, *beg* to be forgiven. In doing so, you deepen your conviction that you are a bad despicable creature who can only be raised up if the other person forgives you. Whether or not you are forgiven is not the most important feature here (although it helps if you are not, of course). What is important is that, by begging for forgiveness, you are acting on the belief that you are a bad person for what you have done and will remain a bad person if you are not forgiven.

Promise unrealistically not to 'sin' again

After you have wronged, harmed or hurt someone and have made yourself feel guilty about doing so (by following the guidelines outlined so far in this chapter), one way to attempt to make yourself feel better in the short term is to promise the other person that you will not 'sin' again. Guilt-wise, you can't lose with this strategy. If the person accepts your promise, you will feel mightily relieved, but in all probability you won't take steps to put your promise into practice by seeking help to address the factors that led you to 'sin' in the first place – indeed, if you are to tempted to do this, resist the temptation. Consequently, you will probably 'sin' again if you encounter these factors, and if you do you will probably make yourself feel guilty for your behaviour all over again. On the other hand, if the person does not accept your promise, you will not gain this short-term relief and will continue to make yourself feel guilty about your 'sin'.

Deprive yourself

When you make yourself feel guilty, think that you don't deserve any good things in life. To reinforce this view, deprive yourself of the good things in life. Don't see your friends, for example, and don't engage in any pleasurable activities. Remind yourself, if you need to, that the reason you are depriving yourself is that as a person you do not deserve such pleasure because of what you have done or failed to do.

Punish yourself

A more extreme version of depriving yourself is punishing yourself. Here, you are not just saying that you do not deserve good things in your life, you are also saying that you deserve bad things in your life. To reinforce this view, it is important that you actively seek out such bad things. For example, you may wish to seek out and spend time with people who actively dislike you, or you may wish to engage in tasks that you actively dislike. In doing so, remind yourself that because of your 'sin' you deserve to be treated badly by the people who dislike you, and you are only fit to engage in the hated tasks.

Do penance

When you are punishing yourself for your 'sin', you are saying that because you are bad you deserve to experience bad things. However, when you do penance for your 'sin' (e.g. deliberately undertaking something onerous) you are saying that you can redeem yourself from your badness by your penance. In doing so, you still hold the belief that you are a bad person for your 'sin'; thus, doing penance, while not as effective at getting your guilt juice flowing as self-punishment, will still help to maintain your guilt-based irrational beliefs, and therefore is well worth considering.

Disclaim responsibility

When you have done something wrong, failed to do the right thing or have caused harm or hurt to someone, and you hold a guilt-inducing irrational belief about your 'sin', you will tend to make yourself guilty. I say 'tend to' here, as you can still stop yourself from feeling guilty before your guilt takes a hold. You can do this by disclaiming responsibility for your actions. Basically, you can do this in two ways. First, you can place the responsibility on some external factor. This might be another person (e.g. 'Yes, I did let you down, but it was my brother's fault. He made me do it') or some aspect of the environment (e.g. 'I would have helped you out, but the train was delayed'). Second, you can place the responsibility on some internal factor like illness or medication (e.g. 'I don't know what came over me. It must have been the medication I am on'). Don't be concerned if by using these excuses you don't actually experience feelings of guilt, for you are still rehearsing your guilt-inducing irrational beliefs, albeit implicitly. For example, when you try to convince yourself that the reason you let down the other person was due to your brother, you are implicitly saying: 'If I acknowledge that I was responsible for letting the other person down, then I would be a bad person. Therefore, to stop blaming myself, I will blame someone else.'

Overcompensate for feelings of guilt

Another way of coping with your feelings of guilt is to overcompensate for them. This involves you doing the very opposite of what you feel guilty about. This technique is worth considering because it does strengthen your guilt-inducing irrational belief. Thus, if you think that you are a bad person for upsetting your friend, you may overcompensate for guilt feelings by going out of your way to be nice to people. You do this because you think that the only way you can get away from the belief that you are bad is by doing good. If you practise such overcompensation, be sure to remind yourself that you are a bad person before you try to be good again by doing good works. Don't use this technique if you succeed in convincing yourself that you are a good person because you have made up for what you have done by doing good deeds. Do employ it if, on the other hand, you still believe that the good deeds you have done do not make up for the harm that you caused, for which you are still a bad person.

Try to get reassurance from others, but fail to be reassured

After you have made yourself guilty for your 'sin', then you may be tempted to go around and ask people for reassurance that what you did wasn't wrong, that there was a good reason for what you did, or that you weren't really responsible for your actions. You will find plenty of people to give you such reassurance, but the good news is that you won't stay reassured for long. Believing that you are a bad person for doing what you absolutely should not have done means that you are not reassurable even if an army of volunteers are recruited to reassure you. For soon after the other person has convinced you that what you did was not wrong, your guilt-inducing irrational belief will lead you to go back to: 'But it was wrong', and from there it is an easy step back to making yourself feel guilty: 'Since it was wrong, I absolutely should not have done it, and because I did, I am a bad person.' The same process happens when the other person convinces you for the moment that there was a good reason for what you did, or that you weren't really responsible for your actions. Here, as before, your guilt-inducing irrational belief will lead you to go back and say to yourself: 'But there really wasn't a good reason for my behaviour' or 'But I am responsible for my actions', and so back to guilt you go when you again evaluate what you did with your guilt-inducing irrational belief.

So when you make yourself guilty, don't be concerned if you go around seeking reassurance. You won't believe any reassurance you are given, and when you re-focus on your 'sin', as you undoubtedly will, your guilt-inducing irrational belief will ensure that a return to guilt will be swift.

Develop and rehearse general guilt-based irrational beliefs

General guilt-based irrational beliefs are irrational beliefs that you hold in many theme-related situations and which enable you to experience guilt in these situations. If you develop and rehearse such beliefs, you will enable yourself to experience guilt in many different situations. You will do this mainly because you will become skilled at inferring that, for example, you have broken your moral or ethical code, failed to live up to your moral or ethical code or caused harm or hurt to relevant others.

Let me show you how this works. First, you need to develop general guilt-based irrational beliefs such as: 'I must never cause hurt or harm to those that I care about and if I do then this proves that I am a bad person.' Now, if you rehearse these beliefs until you firmly believe them and you bring them to relevant situations where it is possible that you cause harm or hurt to relevant others, then because you cannot convince yourself that you will not harm or hurt the other person, you will tend to think that you have harmed or hurt that person. Having created this guilt-based inference, then evaluate it using a specific version of this general guilt-based irrational belief and thereby make yourself feel guilty in the specific situation.

Let me give you a concrete example of how to do this. Develop the following general guilt-based irrational belief: 'I must not upset my mother and if I do I am a bad person.' Imagine taking this belief to a specific situation where your mother asks you over for dinner and you say no because you are going out with a friend that night. You explain this to her, and you are not sure how she has taken the news. Your general guilt-based irrational belief will lead you to infer that you have upset your mother. It is as if you reason: 'Because I can't convince myself that I didn't upset my mother, therefore I did.' Your belief does not allow you to think that your mother was probably OK with you declining her invitation. Once you have

70

created your inference, it is fairly easy to make yourself feel guilty about it by evaluating it with a specific version of your general irrational belief – thus, 'I upset my mother by turning down her dinner invitation. I absolutely should not have upset my mother in this way and I am a bad person because I did.' Having made yourself feel guilty in this way, the next step is to act and think in ways that are consistent with your guilt, and that will strengthen your conviction in guilt-based irrational belief, which will again put the icing on your guilt cake.

Develop and rehearse a view of the world founded on guilt-based irrational beliefs

I mentioned in the previous chapter that people develop world views that render them vulnerable to particular unhealthy negative emotions. The world views that render you vulnerable to guilt do so again because they make it very easy for you to make guilt-related inferences. Then, as I have shown you earlier in this chapter, you make yourself guilty about these inferences with the appropriate irrational beliefs. Here is an illustrative list of guilt-related world views for you to develop and rehearse, together with the inferences that they spawn.

World view: Other people's desires are more important than mine

Inference: If I put my desires first I am being selfish.

World view: I have responsibility for the hurt feelings of others

Inference: If someone's feelings are hurt and I have been involved, then I have hurt that person's feelings.

World view: In the moral domain, I expect more of myself than I do of others

Inference: There is no excuse for what I did.

I hope you can see how you can become really adept at creating guilt feelings for yourself. I will now move on to teach you how to become really adept at making yourself feel unhealthily angry.

5

How to Make Yourself Feel Unhealthily Angry

Unhealthy anger is a particularly destructive emotion, but one that may lead you to feel strong and powerful. This is great news for you because you can make yourself disturbed and enjoy yourself at the same time. Once again I will first outline the general steps that you need to take to make yourself feel unhealthily angry before discussing each step in some detail.

Before I do so, let me discuss terminology again. Unfortunately, we don't have very good words to discriminate between unhealthy and healthy anger so I will use these two terms here, and of course my goal is to teach you how to make yourself unhealthily angry, not healthily so. By *unhealthy anger* (towards another, in this case) I mean a state where you demand that the other person must or must not act in a certain way and where you condemn them for their actions. Your inclination is to attack the person in some way, and you think that they had malevolent intent towards you in their actions in the absence of substantiating evidence. By contrast, *healthy anger* is a state where you would prefer the other person to act or not act in a certain way. You evaluate their behaviour as bad, but do not condemn them for their actions. Your inclination is to confront the other person assertively without attacking them, and you don't necessarily think that they had malevolent intent towards you in their behaviour unless it was clear that this was the case. As you can see, healthy anger is far too constructive a response and should be avoided at all costs. If you follow the advice that follows, fortunately you should avoid falling into the boring healthy anger trap.

How to make yourself unhealthily angry: general steps

The steps that you need to take to make yourself unhealthily angry should be familiar to you by now, since they are the same as I outlined in the previous chapters. Just to refresh your memory, here they are as applied to unhealthy anger.

1 Make an inference about what you are focusing on.

73

2 Appraise that inference using unhealthy anger-based irrational beliefs.
3 Think in ways that are consistent with unhealthy anger-based irrational beliefs.
4 Act in ways that are consistent with these irrational beliefs.
5 Rehearse a general version of your specific unhealthy anger-based irrational beliefs so that you can become skilled at making unhealthy anger-based inferences about what is generally going on in your life.
6 Develop and rehearse an unhealthy anger-based world view.

Now let me deal with these issues one at a time. As I do so, I will concentrate on helping you to make yourself feel unhealthy anger towards others. What I say, however, can easily be generalized so that you can make yourself feel unhealthy anger towards yourself and towards life conditions.

Make unhealthy anger-related inferences

To feel angry, first make one or more inferences about what is going on in your life. Once again, these inferences don't have to reflect accurately what happened. The important point is that you have to believe that they are true. Here is a list of common unhealthy anger-related inferences:

Another person (or group of people) transgressing a socially agreed rule, a legal rule or my own rule

There are socially agreed rules for behaviour, legal rules for behaviour and individuals' own rules about the people they come into contact with. Here are some examples of others transgressing the above rules:

- someone smoking in a non-smoking environment (person breaks socially agreed rule);
- someone driving through a red light (person breaks legal rule);
- someone turning up late for an appointment with me (person breaks individual's rule).

Being blocked or frustrated in my progress towards a goal

As humans, we all have goals that we strive to achieve. Being blocked or frustrated in our pursuit of our goals often serves as an activating event for unhealthy anger. Here are a few examples:

- being stuck in a traffic jam;
- another person blocking my promotion;
- missing a train connection.

Injustice/unfairness

The idea of being treated unjustly or unfairly is a theme that often is found in people's descriptions of episodes of unhealthy anger. In addition, you can make yourself unhealthily angry about injustice or unfairness that has befallen others. Here are a few examples of each:

- being promised a rise if I work overtime, but not receiving it even though I kept my side of the bargain;
- being prosecuted for a crime that I did not commit;
- another person being prosecuted for a crime that they did not commit;
- a child being shouted at unfairly by a parent.

Threats to self-esteem

As I will discuss later in this chapter, there is a distinction between unhealthy ego anger and unhealthy non-ego anger. In unhealthy ego anger, you make yourself unhealthily angry about events that impinge on your self-esteem. Here are a number of such events:

- rejection;
- being criticized;
- being ridiculed.

Being treated without respect

Being treated with disrespect may be a stimulus for you to make yourself unhealthily angry in both ego and non-ego domains.

Hold and rehearse irrational beliefs about your unhealthy anger-related inference

When you make yourself unhealthily angry, you often state or imply that what happened to you (or your inferences about what happened to you) made you unhealthily angry (e.g. 'missing the bus made me furious' or 'your criticism of me made me angry'). Once again you would be wrong, for it is not what happened to you or your inferences about that which make you feel disturbed: rather, you feel disturbed because of the irrational beliefs that you hold about the inferences you make. In this context, you will not feel unhealthily angry about being frustrated, about others transgressing your rules or about being rejected or criticized, for example, without holding irrational beliefs about these inferences.

So let me teach you how to feel unhealthily angry by showing you which irrational beliefs to develop and rehearse about the above inferences.

Before I do so, I want to make an important distinction between two types of unhealthy anger: unhealthy ego anger and unhealthy non-ego anger. When you make yourself unhealthily angry in the ego domain you are angry at someone who, for example, has threatened your self-esteem in some way where at some level you engage in self-depreciation. By contrast, when you make yourself unhealthily angry in the non-ego domain, you are angry at someone who, for example, has acted in some way that you find offensive but that does not pose a threat to your self-esteem and where you do not engage in self-depreciation. To complicate matters a little, it is possible for you to make yourself unhealthily angry in both ego and non-ego domains about the same event. Don't worry too much about this complexity, for the good news is that you have double the opportunity to make yourself unhealthily angry.

So, if what happens to you or your inference about what happens to you does not make you unhealthily angry, what does? The missing link, as with the other disturbed emotions I am teaching in this book, is your irrational beliefs about actual events or your inferences about these events.

What irrational beliefs do you have to hold and rehearse in order to make yourself experience unhealthy ego anger? The following three should do the trick:

1 a rigid demand (e.g. 'You must not criticize me');
2 a self-depreciation belief (e.g. 'Your criticism makes me stupid');
3 an other-depreciation belief (e.g. 'You are a bad person for criticizing me *and for reminding me that I am stupid*' – the section in italics is very implicit and you need to make sure you include it to ensure that your unhealthy anger is ego in nature).

And how can you make yourself unhealthy angry in the non-ego domain? By holding and rehearsing the following irrational beliefs:

1 a rigid demand (e.g. 'I must get to my meeting on time');
2 a low frustration tolerance (LFT) belief (e.g. 'If I don't get to my meeting on time I couldn't bear it'); and either
3 an other-depreciation belief (e.g. 'You are rotten for blocking me from getting to my meeting in time') if one or more other people are involved; or
4 a life-conditions depreciation belief (e.g. 'Conditions are rotten for blocking me from getting to my meeting on time').

I will now take the above and show you how you can apply it to make yourself unhealthily angry about the inferences that I discussed earlier in the chapter. In doing so, I will outline the general irrational belief involved and illustrate it with a specific example.

How to make yourself unhealthily angry about other(s) transgressing socially agreed rules, legal rules and your own personal rules

In general, to make yourself unhealthily angry about another person transgressing a socially agreed rule, a legal rule or one of your own rules, you need to hold a rigid demand about such a transgression:

- The person must not smoke in a non-smoking environment (person breaks socially agreed rule).
- The person absolutely should not have driven through a red light (person breaks legal rule).
- The person absolutely should not have turned up late for an appointment with you (person breaks your own personal rule).

In addition, there is usually an other-depreciation belief about it (here you might find it useful to rate the person as a whole on the basis of their behaviour). Please excuse my language here (but the real language employed by those who are depreciating others is not necessarily polite). However, I will tone it down a little for the sake of good taste.

- The person who is smoking in a non-smoking environment is a selfish sod (person breaks socially agreed rule).
- The person who drove through the red light is an inconsiderate bastard (person breaks legal rule).
- The person is a swine for turning up late for that appointment with you (person breaks individual's rule).

A really good way to ensure that you increase your unhealthy anger about these transgressions is to hold the additional belief: 'Not only must you not break this rule in the first place, but you must not get away with it without being punished in the second place; if you do, then that is unfair and I can't stand you for getting away with this unfairness, and I can't bear the world for allowing you to get away with it.' I will return to this theme of unfairness later in the chapter and show you how to make yourself unhealthily angry about the injustices and unfairness of life.

How to make yourself unhealthily angry about being blocked or frustrated in your progress towards a goal

To make yourself unhealthily angry about being blocked or frustrated in your progress towards a goal, hold a rigid demand and an LFT belief. In cases where you consider that another person is responsible for blocking your path towards your goal, you can make yourself unhealthily angry towards them by additionally holding an other-depreciation belief. Alternatively, in other cases where you consider that you are responsible for the frustration, make yourself unhealthily angry at yourself by additionally holding a self-depreciation belief.

- 'I must not be stuck in the traffic jam (rigid demand) and I can't stand it that I am (LFT belief). Whoever is responsible for this is a bastard (other-depreciation belief).'
- 'Fred blocked my promotions. He absolutely should not have done this (rigid demand) and he is a swine for doing so (other-depreciation belief).'
- 'I missed my train connection because I left home too late. I absolutely should not have done this (rigid demand) and I am an idiot for doing so (self-depreciation belief).'

How to make yourself unhealthily angry about injustice or unfairness

In general, in order to make yourself unhealthily angry about injustice or unfairness you once again need to hold a rigid demand and an LFT belief about such a situation and a depreciation belief against the person, people or organization you deem to be responsible for the injustice/unfairness.

- 'I was promised a rise if I worked overtime. I worked overtime but was not given the promised rise. My boss absolutely should not be so unfair to me (rigid demand). It is intolerable (LFT belief) and he is a bastard for breaking his promise (other-depreciation belief).'
- 'I was prosecuted for a crime that I did not commit. The justice system stinks for doing something to me (depreciation belief about life conditions) that it absolutely should not have done (rigid demand).'
- 'A colleague of mine was prosecuted for a crime that she did not commit. The police are bastards (other-depreciation belief) for doing something to her that they absolutely should not have been allowed to get away with (rigid demand). I can't tolerate this injustice (LFT belief).'

How to make yourself unhealthily angry about a threat to your self-esteem

In order to make yourself unhealthily angry about a threat to your self-esteem, hold three irrational beliefs:

- a rigid demand about the person threatening your self-esteem;
- an other-depreciation belief about this person;
- a self-depreciation belief (usually well hidden) which renders you vulnerable to the threat in the first place.

Let me give you an example to show you how you can put this into practice.

Let's suppose that someone has criticized you. In order to make yourself unhealthily angry about this you need to do the following:

1 Depreciate yourself about this criticism by holding the following irrational belief: 'I must not be criticized and if I am it proves that I am an inadequate person.'
2 Quickly cover up your feelings of inadequacy by holding the person who criticized you responsible for your feelings and depreciate them, as in the following irrational belief: 'You must not criticize me and remind me that I am an inadequate person and you are no good for doing so.'

How to make yourself unhealthily angry about being treated without respect

To make yourself unhealthily angry about being treated with disrespect, you first need to determine whether or not the issue is ego-based or non-ego-based. If the issue is ego-based, you can make yourself unhealthily angry by taking the following steps:

1 Rehearse the irrational belief that the other person must treat you with respect and that if they don't this proves that you are not worthy of respect.
2 Rehearse the irrational belief that the other person must not treat you with disrespect and that by doing so they are reminding you that you are not worthy of respect, and that they are a bastard for so reminding you.

If the issue is non-ego-based, your major concern is that the other person has transgressed your rule for being treated with respect. Thus, in order to make yourself unhealthily angry about this, take the following step:

● Rehearse the irrational belief that the other person must not treat you with disrespect and that they are a bastard for so doing.

Think in ways that are consistent with your unhealthy anger-based irrational beliefs

When you hold an unhealthy anger-creating irrational belief about any of the factors I discussed earlier in this chapter (see pp. 74–5), this belief will influence the way that you subsequently think. If you practise these forms of thinking then you will develop your ability to make yourself unhealthily angry. So when you begin to experience unhealthy anger, think in some of the following ways:

Overestimate the extent to which the other person acted deliberately and with malice towards you

After you have made yourself unhealthily angry, for example about the wrong that another person has done you, and you think about what that person has done, conclude, first, that they acted deliberately in that way towards you (rather than accidentally or because they saw things differently from you) and second, that their behaviour was motivated with malicious intent. It may well be that

80

you thought that way originally and that this was a central feature of what you were unhealthily angry about, but if not, convince yourself that the person was deliberately out to get you. Once you do so, dwell on this inference through the lens of your rigid demand and other depreciation beliefs, then add the idea that you must exact revenge; this should keep you going for quite a long time in the unhealthy anger stakes!

View yourself as definitely right and the other person as definitely wrong

Imagine that you have made yourself unhealthily angry about different versions that you and someone else had of an event. Your unhealthy anger-creating irrational belief will strengthen you in the idea that you were in the right and that the other person was in the wrong. Focus on this, and then tell yourself that the other person absolutely should not have been wrong in the first place, and as you attempt to persuade them that you were right and they were wrong, tell yourself that they must listen to reason and that you must succeed in persuading them of this fact.

Refuse to see the other person's point of view

If you want to diffuse unhealthy anger in someone else, one good way of doing so is to communicate to that person that you understand things from their point of view. An interesting by-product of doing this is that you will lose your own unhealthy anger. So, in order to remain unhealthily angry, it is important that you resist any impulse that you have to see the other person's point of view. Holding an unhealthy anger-creating irrational belief will help prevent you from doing this, as will seeing the other person as being wrong and therefore not worthy of consideration.

Develop and rehearse revenge fantasies

Your imagination is a powerful tool when it comes to making yourself disturbed, and it will help you to remain disturbed as well. One way of holding on to your unhealthy anger and strengthening the irrational beliefs that underpin it is to use your imagination to develop and rehearse revenge fantasies. What you do is the following:

1 Focus on a situation, for example where another person has wronged you.

2 Rehearse your unhealthy anger-creating irrational belief: for example, 'He absolutely should not have wronged me and he is a bastard for so doing.'
3 Show yourself that justice has to be achieved and that you have to get your revenge.
4 Think of ways of getting revenge and develop scenarios where you see yourself in your mind's eye, exacting revenge on the person who has wronged you.
5 Focus on the delicious sense of pleasure you get when seeing yourself, in your mind's eye, exacting revenge.

Every time you rehearse a revenge fantasy you strengthen your conviction in the following two anger-creating irrational beliefs:

• The other person is bad for doing what they absolutely should not have done to you.
• When someone has wronged you, you must get your own back and punish that person.

Carefully nurtured, these two irrational beliefs will give you a lifetime of unhealthy anger!

Act in ways that are consistent with your unhealthy anger-based irrational beliefs

If you have followed and implemented what I have said so far, you should now be able to make yourself feel unhealthily angry. The next step is to maintain and even deepen this unhealthy emotion by acting in ways that are consistent with your unhealthy anger-based irrational beliefs. As I have noted before, the great thing about engaging in such behaviours is that doing so helps to reinforce and strengthen your conviction in your unhealthy anger-creating irrational beliefs, so engage in as many as you can.

Verbally blame the other person for making you unhealthily angry

When discussing your unhealthily angry feelings with friends and acquaintances, it is useful to place the blame verbally for your angry feelings on the behaviour of the person with whom you are unhealthily angry. Taking responsibility for making yourself unhealthily angry is the first step to overcome these feelings, so we definitely don't want you to do that. Rather, place the blame verbally on the other person for making you angry and you won't be tempted to take steps to overcome such unhealthy feelings but will help to perpetuate them.

Attack the other person verbally

After you have made yourself unhealthily angry, for example about what another person has done to you, you will feel an urge to attack them verbally. If you want to deepen your conviction in your unhealthy anger-creating irrational belief, act on this urge and shout and scream at the other person. When you do this, one of two things will happen. First, the other person may make themselves unhealthily angry about your verbal attack and attack you back. This is good because you can then make yourself unhealthily angry about their verbal attack, and so on and so forth. Second, the other person may display signs that they feel hurt about your behaviour. This then gives you an opportunity to practise making yourself feel guilty for hurting their feelings (see Chapter 4).

Pursue revenge

Revenge is sweet, and pursuing it will certainly help to strengthen your unhealthy anger-related irrational beliefs. Thus you can enjoy yourself at the same time as you disturb yourself: two pleasures for the price of one. When you pursue revenge directly (by which I mean that the other person knows that it is you who has meted out revenge) you not only hold the belief that the other person absolutely should not have wronged you in the way they did, you also hold one or more of the following irrational beliefs, which you should learn and practise at every possible opportunity:

- 'The other person absolutely must not get away with their bad behaviour towards me.'
- 'The wrong towards me must be put right.'
- 'They must be punished for their behaviour towards me.'
- 'I must be the one to punish the other person and they must know that it was me who did it.'

Attack the other person passive–aggressively

Gaining revenge can also be achieved indirectly. This is known as passive–aggressive behaviour and is another good way to reinforce your unhealthy anger-creating irrational beliefs. When you are passive–aggressive in your attacks, you get revenge against the other person, but while they know that someone has attacked them, they don't realize who has attacked them. As such you are acting on the following irrational beliefs:

- 'The other person absolutely must not get away with their bad behaviour towards me.'
- 'The wrong towards me must be put right.'
- 'They must be punished for their behaviour towards me, but they must not know that I am the person who has attacked them.'

Recruit allies against the other person

Another good way of paying someone back (and strengthening your conviction in your unhealthy anger-creating irrational beliefs) is to recruit allies against the other person. This may involve you recruiting people to engage in a direct vengeful attack on the other, to deprive that person of their place in a social group or to besmirch the reputation of that person in the social community. In all three cases you will be acting on the irrational belief that the person absolutely should not have wronged you or your reference group, is a bad person for so doing and thereby deserves to be paid back for their behaviour.

Express your unhealthy anger cathartically

The counselling and psychotherapy field used to think that it was healthy to express your unhealthy anger, and that if you didn't then you would turn your anger towards yourself and make yourself feel depressed. If this were really the case then I certainly would not recommend that you openly express your unhealthy anger. However, we now know that expressing your unhealthy anger cathartically (i.e. with fully expressed feeling) only serves to make you even angrier (in the unhealthy sense). This is because as you express your unhealthy anger you are rehearsing and thereby reinforcing your unhealthy anger-creating irrational beliefs. The answer to the question: 'How do you get to Carnegie Hall?' is 'Practise, practise, practise'. Similarly, the answer to the question: 'How do you make yourself unhealthily angry?' is 'Practise, practise, practise'. One great way to practise is to express your anger cathartically.

Displace your unhealthy anger or 'kick the cat'

You have probably heard the phrase 'kicking the cat'. This refers to times when you take your unhealthy anger out on an innocent bystander. Doing so serves to reinforce your unhealthy anger-related irrational beliefs in a similar way to cathartic expression of unhealthy anger. When you 'kick the cat' you are expressing your unhealthy anger indirectly at the person with whom you have a problem. You do not express your unhealthy anger feelings directly at the person for a number of reasons, with anxiety heading the list. So if you are unhealthily angry at someone to whom you cannot express your angry feelings directly, express these feelings to someone who won't answer back. Deliberately rehearsing your unhealthy angry-creating irrational belief as you do so will also help to perpetuate your anger problem.

Withdraw aggressively

A final way of strengthening your unhealthy anger-creating irrational beliefs and thus making yourself more prone to unhealthy anger is to withdraw aggressively from situations in which you have made yourself unhealthily angry. There are two major ways of withdrawing aggressively when you are unhealthily angry. The first is to leave situations in which you feel unhealthy anger, demonstrating non-verbally that you are unhealthily angry. Brian, for example, used to make himself unhealthily angry in business meetings and storm out of these meetings, banging the door as strongly as he could. Don't worry that you may get into trouble with your boss, as Brian did: just focus on the pleasure that withdrawing aggressively brings, as well as the knowledge that you are refining your ability to make yourself unhealthily angry.

Develop and rehearse general unhealthy anger-based irrational beliefs

The next step in furthering your competence at making yourself unhealthily angry is developing and rehearsing general unhealthy anger-based irrational beliefs. General unhealthy anger-based irrational beliefs are irrational beliefs that you hold in many theme-related situations, which enable you to experience unhealthy anger in these situations. If you develop and rehearse such beliefs, you will enable yourself to experience unhealthy anger in many different situations. You will do this mainly because you will become skilled at inferring, for example, that others have transgressed socially agreed, legal or your own personal rules, that others have frustrated your goal-directed efforts, that others have behaved unjustly or unfairly to you and/or others, and that others are posing a threat to your self-esteem.

Let me show you how this works. First, you need to develop a general unhealthy anger-based irrational belief such as: 'Other people must obey the rules and they are rotten people if they don't.' Now, if you rehearse this general belief until you firmly believe it and you bring it to relevant situations where it is possible that others may not obey the rules, then because you cannot convince yourself that they will not obey the rules you will tend to think that they have disobeyed the rules, and that they have done so deliberately and with malicious intent. Having created this unhealthy anger-based inference, you will then evaluate it using a specific version of this general unhealthy anger-based irrational belief, and will thereby make yourself feel unhealthy anger in the specific situation.

Let me give you a concrete example of how to do this. Develop the following general unhealthy anger-based irrational belief: 'Others must respect me, and if they don't I am not worthy of respect and they are no good for showing this'. Imagine taking this belief to a specific situation where you are in a restaurant with a group of friends, and a waiter asks everybody else for their order but doesn't ask you for yours. Your general unhealthy anger-based irrational belief will lead you to infer that the waiter showed you disrespect by not asking for your order. It is as if you reason: 'Because I can't convince myself that his failing to ask me for my order was an innocent mistake, then he did show me disrespect.' Your belief does not allow you to think that the waiter may have made a mistake. Once you have created your inference that you have been treated disrespectfully, it is fairly easy to make yourself feel unhealthy anger about it by evaluating it with a specific version of your general irrational belief, thus: 'The waiter treated me disrespectfully me by not asking me for my order. He absolutely should have shown me respect, and because he didn't I am not a person worthy of respect, and he is no good for proving this.'

Having made yourself feel unhealthy anger in this way, the next step is to act and think in ways that are consistent with your unhealthy anger and that will strengthen your conviction in your unhealthy anger-based irrational belief, and this will again put the icing on your unhealthy anger cake.

Develop and rehearse a view of the world based on unhealthy anger-based irrational beliefs

I mentioned earlier in this book that people develop world views that render them vulnerable to particular unhealthy negative emotions. This is certainly the case with unhealthy anger. The world views that render you vulnerable to unhealthy anger do so primarily because they make it very easy for you to make unhealthy anger-related inferences. Then, as I have shown you earlier in this chapter, you make yourself unhealthily angry about these inferences with the appropriate irrational beliefs. Here is an illustrative list of world views for you to develop and rehearse, together with the inferences that they spawn.

World view: *It's a dog-eat-dog world*

Inference: People's actions will often be vicious and attacking.

World view: *People only look after themselves and their own*

Inference: People's motives are primarily influenced by selfishness.

World view: *There's no such thing as an accident. People always act with deliberation*

Inference: When people transgress the rules they do so deliberately.

World view: *People are out to get me, so I need to get them before they get me*

Inference: People's actions are designed to harm me.

I hope you can see how you can become really adept at creating unhealthy anger for yourself. I will now move on to teach you how to become really adept at making yourself feel hurt.

6

How to Make Yourself Feel Hurt

Feeling hurt is an unhealthy negative emotion that you are most likely to experience about the way that people significant to you behave (or fail to behave). I will follow the usual format in this chapter by first outlining the general steps that you need to take to make yourself feel unhealthily hurt before discussing each step in some detail.

How to make yourself feel hurt: general steps

The steps that you need to take to make yourself feel hurt will now be familiar to you if you have read the foregoing chapters. Here they are as applied to feeling hurt.

1 Make an inference about what you are focusing on.
2 Appraise that inference using hurt-based irrational beliefs.
3 Think in ways that are consistent with the above irrational beliefs.
4 Act in ways that are consistent with these irrational beliefs.
5 Rehearse a general version of your specific hurt-based irrational beliefs so that you can become skilled at making hurt-based inferences about what is generally going on in your life.
6 Develop and rehearse a hurt-based world view.

Now let me deal with these issues one at a time.

Make hurt-related inferences

In order to feel hurt you first need to make one or more inferences about what is going on in your life. As I have repeatedly stressed, these inferences don't have to reflect accurately what happened. The important point is that you have to believe that they are true. What people tend to feel hurt about is what others (usually significant others) have done or have failed to do. What follows is a list of common hurt-related inferences about what people have done. It is

89

important to note that the person feeling hurt considers that they do not deserve such behaviour at the hands of the other person. Indeed, it is very likely that the person considers that they deserve the very opposite.

Being unfairly criticized

While you can feel hurt about fair or unfair criticism, you are more likely to feel hurt about a significant other criticizing you unfairly. In addition, you are more likely to feel hurt about criticism that is directed to you as a person rather than criticism that is directed at your behaviour. Given these points, seek out people you are close to who are likely to criticize you unfairly as a person. Don't despair if you can only get fair criticism of your behaviour. In these circumstances, think that even such criticism is undeserved.

Being rejected

To feel hurt about being rejected, focus on the undeserved nature of the rejection. Remind yourself of all the good things you have done for the person and how you deserve far better. In order to be rejected, you need to set up situations where you ask for things at very inconvenient times for the other person. Then forget about the fact that your request is unreasonable and focus on the fact that you have been rejected and on how you don't deserve to be rejected. Indeed, focus on how much you deserve to get what you asked for. For example, make sexual overtures at a time when your partner is very unlikely to respond. Forget about the untimeliness of your request, and instead tell yourself that you have gone to a lot of trouble to make life pleasant for your partner and the least you deserve is some pleasure in return.

Being disapproved of by the other person

Disapproval is similar to rejection in that they both involve the other person making some kind of negative judgement of you, but they are different in that in rejection the other person has cast you aside, which they haven't done yet when they disapprove of you. To maximize the conditions for feeling hurt about being disapproved of, seek out disapproval from someone you anticipate will approve of you, on an issue where you don't think you deserve to be disapproved of.

Being betrayed by the other

Being betrayed by someone you are close to is a key hurt-related inference. A good way to consider that you have been betrayed by someone significant close to you is to do the following. Place absolute trust in people close to you and then tell them all a secret, making them all swear not to tell a living soul. Chances are that someone will tell another person about your secret and, people being people, you will find out about it. This will give you great ammunition to feel hurt, the next step of which is to focus on the fact that you have been betrayed by someone close to you.

The next list of hurt-related inferences concerns what other people fail to do. Once again, it is important to note that the person feeling hurt is likely to consider that they deserve far better treatment than they are getting from the other person.

Being neglected

Inferring that you have been neglected by someone close to you is a common hurt-related inference. If you don't think that you are being neglected by any of your significant others, this is how to go about encouraging others to neglect you. First, for example, take the lead with all of your friends in making social arrangements, and continue to do this for a long period until your friends have grown used to the idea that you will do it in future. Then suddenly stop making such arrangements without explaining why, and wait for others to take over the reins of social secretary and contact you about such arrangements. When they don't (and they won't for a while because they are waiting for you to do your 'usual' job) remind yourself that you are being neglected by your friends, and that after all you have done for them you don't deserve such neglect.

Being unfairly excluded

Being unfairly excluded by a significant other when you think you don't deserve to be is a common situation about which people make themselves feel hurt. Particularly good situations to seek out here involve three-person situations, where all are friends but two of the people have more in common than the third. It goes without saying that you should ensure that you are the third person in this unbalanced triangle. In order to maximize the hurt potential in this situation, it is important you think that you deserve to get equal attention from the two other people and that it is unfair for them to speak to each other for a lengthy period of time and exclude you. It is also helpful if you stay silent for significant periods, to encourage them to talk to one another.

Not being appreciated

Not being appreciated when you deserve to be is another good situation where you can make yourself feel hurt. What you do is to choose someone you are close to who is particularly unappreciative, and then do a lot for them. When they don't show their appreciation, focus on the unfairness of the situation.

Being deprived of what you want when you think you have deserved it

As you have now seen, the concept of deservingness is an important one in situations about which you make yourself feel hurt. You can use this concept and apply it to any situation where you have been deprived of what you want. Take a significant other, focus on something you are not getting from them which you deserve to get, and providing it is something that you want you will feel hurt about this deprivation as long as you bring your hurt-creating philosophy (see below) to this situation.

Develop and rehearse irrational beliefs about your hurt-related inference

You have probably grasped one of the main points of this book by now, which is that in order to make yourself feel emotionally disturbed about something it is necessary to hold a disturbance-creating irrational belief about this 'something'. The corollary of this is that situations, or your inferences about situations, while contributing to your disturbed feelings do not on their own disturb you. Rather, you disturb yourself about these situations (actual or inferred) by your irrational beliefs. Applying this to the topic of hurt, we can say that being unfairly excluded, for example, does not make you feel hurt; rather, you make yourself feel hurt about unfair exclusion by the irrational beliefs that you hold about this actual or inferred event. Let me now discuss what these irrational beliefs are so that you can learn and practise them to help you in your quest to make yourself emotionally disturbed.

Before I do so, I want to make an important distinction between two types of hurt, ego hurt and non-ego hurt. When you make yourself feel hurt in the ego domain, you feel hurt because you are depreciating yourself in some way for undeserved treatment you have experienced at the hands of a significant other. By contrast, when you make yourself feel hurt in the non-ego domain, you are focusing on how horrible the world is for allowing you be treated in such an unfair way. You are not depreciating yourself for this treatment; rather, you feel sorry for yourself for the way you have been treated. To complicate matters, as with unhealthy anger, it is possible for you to make yourself feel hurt in both ego and non-ego domains about the same event. Don't worry too much about this complexity, for the good news is that you have double the opportunity to make yourself feel hurt.

Now let me discuss the irrational beliefs that lead to hurt in both these domains. Let me begin with ego hurt.

Irrational beliefs in ego hurt

To feel ego hurt you need at least two beliefs:

- a rigid demand (e.g. 'You must not reject me');
- a self-depreciation belief (e.g. 'Your rejection makes me unlovable').

Sometimes, when unhealthy anger is a feature of hurt, you also hold an other–depreciation belief (e.g. 'You are rotten for rejecting me since you are reminding me that I am unlovable').

Irrational beliefs in non-ego hurt

And how can you make yourself feel hurt in the non-ego domain? By holding and rehearsing the following irrational beliefs:

- a rigid demand (e.g. 'You must not betray me') and one, two or all of the following:
- an awfulizing belief (e.g. 'It is awful that you betrayed me. Poor me, I don't deserve to be treated like this');
- a low frustration tolerance (LFT) belief (e.g. 'I can't stand being betrayed. Poor me, I don't deserve to be treated like this');

93

- a world-depreciation belief (e.g. 'The world is a rotten place for allowing such bad treatment to poor, undeserving me');
- an other-depreciation belief (e.g. 'You are a bad person for betraying me').This is particularly the case where unhealthy anger is a feature of non-ego hurt.

If you have followed what I have taught you in the previous chapters, you should now be able to take what I have just said about the irrational beliefs in both types of hurt and apply this to the hurt-related inferences discussed earlier.

Think in ways that are consistent with your hurt-based irrational beliefs

As I have discussed with the other unhealthy negative emotions I have been training you to experience, when you hold a hurt-creating irrational belief about any of the factors I discussed earlier in this chapter (see pp. 89–92), this belief will influence the way that you subsequently think. If you practise these forms of thinking, then you will develop your ability to make yourself feel hurt. So when you begin to experience hurt, think in some of the following ways:

Overestimate the unfairness of the other person's behaviour

As I discussed earlier in this chapter, you are much more likely to make yourself feel hurt about being treated badly by those close to you when you consider that you do not deserve such treatment than when you think you do. When you hold hurt-based irrational beliefs and when you think again about the way you have been treated by the other person, your tendency is to overestimate the unfairness in the way you have been treated. Specifically, think about all the good things you have done for the other person and edit out all the good things they have done for you. Consequently, you will dwell on the unfair imbalance that your irrational beliefs encourage you to focus on. If you find yourself thinking in balanced ways about your behaviour towards the other person and their behaviour towards you, desist at once. Instead list all the good things you have done for the other person and compare this with the way in which they have just treated you. This will get you back on the right hurt-based lines.

See the other person as showing indifference or a lack of care

When you hold hurt-based irrational beliefs about the unfair treatment that you have experienced at the hands of someone close to you, conclude that the reason they treated you so badly is that they don't care about you or are indifferent towards you. If you think this way, you will then focus on their indifference or lack of caring, and have the opportunity of disturbing yourself about this attitude by thinking irrationally about it. If you want to make yourself feel hurt about their attitude, follow the guidelines that I have outlined in this chapter. If you want to feel depressed about it, consult Chapter 2.

See yourself as alone, uncared for or misunderstood

When you hold hurt-based irrational beliefs about being mistreated by a significant other, see yourself placed in a negative situation in relation to the world. This view is usually an overgeneralization. So when someone mistreats you, tell yourself that you are alone in the world, uncared for in the world or misunderstood by the world. This negative situation will be coloured by ego-based hurt (e.g. 'I am uncared for in the world. This proves that I am not worth caring about') or by non-ego-based hurt (e.g. 'I am alone in the world. Poor me!').

Think of past 'hurts'

When you have made yourself feel hurt by holding a relevant hurt-based irrational belief, one great way of perpetuating this belief, and thus ensuring many fun-filled hours of feeling hurt in the future, is to focus on past hurts. Your irrational belief encourages you to do this anyway, but it is worth making a deliberate effort to do so nonetheless. You do this by bringing to mind all the occasions you have been mistreated, unappreciated, unfairly rejected, etc., by other people.

Think that the other person has to put things right of their own accord

As we shall see when we discuss sulking, one of the purposes of such behaviour is to encourage the other person to take action of their own accord to put things right between you. Your hurt-based irrational belief will encourage you to think this way, but if not remind yourself that since you were unfairly treated (for example) by the other person, the fair thing for that person to do is to make the first move. Thinking this way will help to strengthen your conviction in your hurt-based irrational belief.

Act in ways that are consistent with your hurt-based irrational beliefs

If you have followed and implemented what I have said so far, you should now be able to make yourself feel hurt. The next step is to maintain and even deepen this unhealthy emotion by acting in ways that are consistent with your hurt-based irrational beliefs. The great thing about engaging in such behaviours is that doing so helps to reinforce and strengthen your conviction in your hurt-creating irrational beliefs, so engage in as many as you can.

Blame the other person for making you feel hurt

As with unhealthy anger, when discussing your feelings of hurt with friends and acquaintances it is useful to place the blame for your hurt feelings on the behaviour of the person with whom you feel hurt. Don't, whatever you do, take responsibility for making yourself feel like this, since doing so will help you to overcome your feelings of hurt, which is the last thing that you want to do. Rather, place the blame on the other person for making you feel hurt and you won't be tempted to take steps to overcome such unhealthy feelings, thus helping to perpetuate them.

Shut down direct channels of communication with the other person, while communicating indirectly that they have 'hurt' you

Perhaps the best way to strengthen your conviction in your hurt-creating irrational beliefs is to shut down direct channels of communication with the person about whom you have made yourself feel hurt. The main point here is not to communicate directly with the person and tell them why you feel hurt. Such a course of action might lead to a fruitful discussion, the result of which might be a resolution of your feelings of hurt. This will not do, so the best thing is not to tell the other person directly how you feel. Does this mean that you cannot *indirectly* show the other person how you feel? Not at all. Indeed, a very good way of maintaining your feelings of hurt is to show the person indirectly that you are in a mood with them. This is commonly known as sulking.

Sulking comes in two major forms. The first involves you not talking to the other person at all. You can either do this loudly (e.g. by banging doors) or quietly (by silently rebuffing all attempts by the other person to engage you in direct communication). The second form of sulking involves you criticizing the other person but not telling them what you feel hurt about.

As I showed in my book *The Incredible Sulk* (Sheldon Press, 1992), sulking has a number of purposes, all of which are consistent with your goal of making yourself feel hurt and sustaining these feelings. The purposes of sulking are as follows:

- to punish the other person for 'hurting' your feelings (this has the added bonus of strengthening your conviction in your unhealthy anger-creating irrational beliefs);
- to get what you want from the other person (if your sulking behaviour works then you will be more likely to use it in future, and thus strengthen your hurt-creating irrational beliefs);
- to get the other person to make the first move (part of the philosophy that underpins feeling hurt is that you have been treated unfairly by the other person, and that it is up to the other person to make efforts to find out how they have 'hurt' you and then to put things right between you; it is also part of this philosophy not to make this process too easy for the other person);
- to extract proof of caring from the other person (here the other person has to prove that they care for you by making continued attempts to get you to talk. If they don't do this or they give up too easily, you have something else to make yourself feel hurt about);
- to protect yourself from further hurt (by doing this you are practising your hurt-creating irrational belief indirectly, for it is as if you are saying: 'I need to stop communicating with this other person because if I continue to communicate with them, they will keep acting in ways that I will feel hurt about. Thus, I'll stop communicating');
- to restore a sense of power (here your sulking is an attempt to get the upper hand in the relationship with the person who, in your mind, has hurt you. In doing so you reinforce your hurt-creating irrational beliefs).

Put these purposes into practice and you will become more proficient at sulking and making yourself feel hurt.

Develop and rehearse general unhealthy hurt-based irrational beliefs

The next step in furthering your competence at making yourself feel hurt is for you to develop and rehearse general hurt-based irrational beliefs. General hurt-based irrational beliefs are irrational beliefs that you hold in many theme-related situations which enable you to experience hurt in these situations. If you develop and rehearse such beliefs, you will enable yourself to experience hurt in a variety of different situations. You will do this mainly because you will become skilled at inferring, for example, that those close to you do not appreciate you or have treated you unfairly.

Let me show you how this works. First, you need to develop a general hurt-based irrational belief (in this case in the non-ego domain) such as: 'Those close to me must include me in everything that they do and it's terrible if they don't. Poor me if I am excluded.' Now, if you rehearse this general belief until you firmly believe it and you bring it to relevant situations where it is possible that others may not include you, then because you cannot convince yourself that they will include you or that there is a good reason for your exclusion, you will tend to think that they have unfairly excluded you and have done so intentionally. Having created this hurt-based inference, you will then evaluate it using a specific version of this general hurt-based irrational belief, thereby making yourself feel hurt in the specific situation.

Let me give you a concrete example of how to do this. Develop the following general hurt-based irrational belief: 'Because I would not betray the trust of those close to me, they must not betray my trust, and if they do the world is a rotten place for allowing this to happen to poor, undeserving me.' Imagine taking this belief to a specific situation where you learn that your sister, whose confidences you have kept in the past, *may* have told a group of your mutual friends, when drunk, something that you told her in strict confidence. Your general hurt-based irrational belief will lead you to infer that she did, in fact, betray your trust. It is as if you reason: 'Because I can't convince myself that my sister did not betray my trust, then she did. If she did so, she betrayed my trust intentionally.' Your belief does not easily allow you to think that your sister did not betray your trust, or that, if she did, she did so unintentionally because she was drunk. Once you have created your inference that you have been betrayed, it is fairly easy to make yourself feel hurt about it by evaluating it with a specific version of your general irrational belief, thus: 'My sister betrayed my trust intentionally by telling our mutual friends something that I told her in confidence. She absolutely should not have betrayed me and the world is a rotten place for allowing this to happen to poor, undeserving me.'

Having made yourself feel hurt in this way, the next step is to act and think in ways that are consistent with your feelings of hurt and that will strengthen your conviction in your hurt-based irrational belief (as discussed earlier in this chapter).

Develop and rehearse a view of the world founded on hurt-based irrational beliefs

I mentioned earlier in this book that people develop world views that render them vulnerable to particular unhealthy negative emotions. The world views that render you vulnerable to feelings of hurt do so primarily because they make it very easy for you to make hurt-related inferences. Then, as I have shown you earlier in this chapter, you make yourself feel hurt about these inferences with the appropriate irrational beliefs. Here is an illustrative list of world views for you to develop and rehearse, together with the inferences that they spawn.

World view: When I do a lot for those close to me, they will fail to reciprocate

Inference: People close to me will let me down.

World view: If I trust those close to me they will often betray me, while I would not betray them

Inference: People close to me will betray me.

World view: Significant others will act unfairly towards me, while I would not be unfair to them

Inference: I will not get what I deserve from significant others.

World view: Those close to me will often exclude or neglect me for no good reason

Inference: If I learn that people close to me are doing things together when I have not been invited, this is evidence that I have been excluded or neglected.

I hope you can see how you can become really adept at creating feelings of hurt. I will now move on to teach you how to become really adept at making yourself feel unhealthily jealous.

7

How to Make Yourself Feel Unhealthily Jealous

Unhealthy jealousy ruins relationships! If you have a problem with unhealthy jealousy (which you will have if you follow the guidelines in this chapter), you will make it very difficult for anyone to have an ongoing love relationship with you. In fact, in order for someone to sustain an ongoing relationship with you, they will have to have the patience of a saint and either low self-esteem or an unhealthy need to help you overcome your jealousy problem. Saints are in short supply these days, so we can rule them out. On the other hand, people with low self-esteem who have a need to help you are in plentiful supply, and at least you have the consolation that you can drive such people mad with your unhealthy jealousy.

Before I teach you how to make yourself unhealthily jealous, let me again discuss terminology. As with anger, we don't have very good words to discriminate between unhealthy and healthy jealousy, so I will use these two terms here. Of course, my goal is to teach you how to make yourself unhealthily jealous, not healthily so. By *unhealthy jealousy* I mean a state where you demand that your partner must only have eyes for you and must not show interest in anyone who you deem to be a love rival. Your inclination is to monitor your partner closely for signs that they are interested in another person; you question them closely to this effect and either check on their whereabouts or restrict their movements. By contrast, *healthy jealousy* is a state where you prefer that your partner only has for you and doesn't show interest in anyone you deem to be a love rival, but you do not insist that this must be the case. Your inclination is to assume that your partner is not interested in another person unless you have clear evidence to the contrary, and if you do you will confront the person with your evidence in a clear, assertive way. You will neither monitor your partner closely for signs that they are interested in another person, question them closely to this effect nor check on their whereabouts or restrict their movements.

As you can see, healthy jealousy is far too constructive a response and should be avoided at all costs. If you follow the advice that follows, you will be able to avoid feeling healthily jealous.

How to make yourself unhealthily jealous: general steps

The steps that you need to take to make yourself unhealthily jealous will be familiar to you by now, since they are the same as those I outlined in the previous chapters. As an overview, here they are as applied to unhealthy jealousy.

1 Make an inference about what you are focusing on.
2 Appraise that inference using unhealthy jealousy-based irrational beliefs.
3 Think in ways that are consistent with the above irrational beliefs.
4 Act in ways that are consistent with these irrational beliefs.
5 Rehearse a general version of your specific unhealthy jealousy-based irrational beliefs so that you can become skilled at making unhealthy jealousy-based inferences about what is generally going on in your life.
6 Develop and rehearse an unhealthy jealousy-based world view.

I will now deal with these issues one at a time. As I do so, I will concentrate on romantic jealousy.

Make unhealthy jealousy-related inferences

To feel unhealthily jealous, first focus on a scenario (which can be real or imagined) which has three people in it: you, your partner and another person who you see as an actual or potential love rival. Then, infer that the other person poses a threat to your relationship with your partner. The nature of this threat is likely to be fivefold. Consequently, follow one or more of the following guidelines:

- *My partner will leave me*
  Regard the other person in the triangle as someone who will replace you in the affections of your partner and think that your partner will leave you for the other person.
- *I'm not the most important person in my partner's life*
  Think that your partner finds the other person more attractive than you and that you will be displaced as the most important person in your partner's life (even though you don't think that they will go off with the other person).

102

- *I'm not my partner's one and only*
  Acknowledge that it is important to you that your partner is only interested in you and that their interest in the other person means that you are no longer their one and only.
- *Someone is showing an interest in my partner*
  Acknowledge that it is important to you that no one (who has the potential to be a love rival) shows an interest in your partner, so when someone does you deem this to be a threat.
- *I don't know what my partner is doing or thinking*
  Focus on the fact that unless you place your partner under constant surveillance (which, of course, you would like to do) you will not know what they are doing. Indeed, even if you do manage to know at all times what your partner is doing, it is unlikely that you will ever know for sure what they are thinking. To become really adept at making yourself unhealthily jealous, seek out and focus on such uncertainty.

As I have mentioned several times, these inferences don't have to reflect accurately what is happening or what has happened. In fact, when you feeling unhealthily jealous it is likely that your inferences are likely to be false. This doesn't matter too much, for the important point is that you have to believe that they are true.

Hold and rehearse irrational beliefs about your unhealthy jealousy-related inferences

You will now not need reminding that your unhealthy jealousy is not caused by your inference that your partner may find someone else attractive, for example. Rather, these unhealthy feelings are determined by the irrational beliefs that you hold about this inference, true or not. So let me teach you how to feel unhealthily jealous by showing you which irrational beliefs to develop and rehearse about the above inferences.

First, focus on the uncertainty of not knowing what your partner is doing at the office party to which you have not been invited. Then hold the following irrational beliefs about this uncertainty, which are in the area of non-ego disturbance (where your problem is not related to your view of yourself):

- a rigid demand (e.g. 'I must know that my partner does not find anyone at the party attractive');

- an LFT belief (e.g. 'I can't stand not knowing that my partner does not find anyone at the party attractive').

As I will discuss later in this chapter, these related irrational beliefs lead you to conclude that under these circumstances your partner does find others at the party attractive and that, for example, this means you are not the one and only person your partner finds attractive. Then focus on this situation and hold and rehearse the following irrational beliefs (which are in the area of ego disturbance, where you depreciate yourself in some way):

- a rigid demand (e.g. 'My partner must find only me attractive');
- a self-depreciation belief (e.g. 'If my partner finds other people attractive this means that I am unattractive and worthless').

You can rehearse similar irrational beliefs about the other inferences I discussed earlier. Thus:

- 'My partner must not leave me. If they do, it proves that I am unlovable.'
- 'I must be the most important person in my partner's life. If I'm not then I am nothing.'
- 'I must be my partner's one and only. If I am not then I am worthless.'

The above irrational beliefs are also an example of ego disturbance.

When you hold an irrational belief about other people showing an interest in your partner, most frequently this is in the area of non-ego disturbance. Thus:

- 'Nobody else must show an interest in my partner. If they do it's terrible;'

or

- 'Nobody else must show an interest in my partner. If they do they are no good.'

Think in ways that are consistent with your unhealthy jealousy-based irrational beliefs

When you hold an unhealthy jealousy-creating irrational belief about any of the factors I discussed earlier in this chapter (see pp. 102–3), this belief will influence the way that you subsequently think. If you practise these forms of thinking then you will develop your ability to make yourself unhealthily jealous, particularly by strengthening your conviction in your irrational belief. So when you begin to experience unhealthy jealousy, think in some of the following ways:

Distrust and be suspicious of your partner

Show yourself that whatever your partner says or does, they are not to be trusted. Indeed, being suspicious and distrustful of your partner (and past and potential partners) is a really important factor if you are to become thoroughly adept at unhealthy jealousy. Thus, look for discrepancies in what your partner says and/or does; keeping a note of their movements will provide you with the necessary ammunition here. When you find a discrepancy, however small, remind yourself that this is evidence that your partner cannot be trusted.

Think of relevant people as love rivals

When you have made yourself unhealthily jealous about your partner in one context, you can perpetuate your unhealthy jealousy problem by thinking that relevant people (e.g. all attractive men) are potential love rivals. This will help you to see that your relationship with your partner is always under threat – one of the main features of a chronic unhealthy jealousy problem.

Think that your partner has a negative attitude towards you

Your unhealthy jealousy-related irrational beliefs will lead you to think that your partner has a negative attitude towards you. Capitalize on this by reminding yourself of all the negative things that they have said about you. This will reinforce the irrational belief that you are not worth caring about.

Think in distorted ways about your partner's behaviour

Once you have made yourself unhealthily jealous about your partner's behaviour (for example, about him – in this case – talking to an attractive woman at a social gathering), thinking in negatively distorted ways about your partner's behaviour will help you to maintain your unhealthy jealous feelings. Thus, in the above example, try thinking one or more of the following:

- He wants to have an affair with her.
- He is betraying me.

- He is rejecting me.
- He is making me look a fool in the eyes of other people.

I hope you can see that thinking in such distorted ways will increase the chances that you will perpetuate your unhealthy jealous feelings, particularly if you evaluate these distortions with your irrational beliefs (e.g. 'By talking to that woman, my partner is rejecting me and this proves that I am worthless').

Think in distorted ways about your future relationships

Having made yourself unhealthily jealous about your present relationship, make sure that you carry your problem with unhealthy jealousy into future relationships by thinking in negatively distorted ways about these relationships. Thus, for example, when you feel unhealthily jealous about your partner's unfaithful behaviour (real or, more likely, imagined), think that any future partners you may have will also act in the same ways and that you will never have a relationship with someone who will be faithful to you. Given that you think all partners will be unfaithful, *in your mind* this will probably be true, even though it will be unlikely in reality!

Think negatively about your own qualities (particularly in relation to possible love rivals)

When you have made yourself unhealthily jealous, you can perpetuate the irrational beliefs that spawned them by thinking negatively about your own qualities. Thus, when you feel unhealthily jealous about your partner talking to an attractive woman, think that by comparison you are unattractive, uninteresting and unintelligent. These negative thoughts will help fuel your self-depreciation beliefs and so increase the chances that you will make yourself unhealthily jealous in the future.

Think positively about the qualities of your love rivals (particularly in relation to yourself)

A companion to thinking negatively about yourself when you are unhealthily jealous is to think positively about the qualities of potential love rivals. Thus, when you feel unhealthily jealous about your partner talking to an attractive woman, think that by comparison she is attractive, interesting and intelligent. These thoughts will also help fuel your self-depreciation beliefs and thus increase the chances that you will make yourself unhealthily jealous in the future.

Best of all, why not combine thinking negatively about yourself with thinking positively about your love rival? In doing so, you double the chances that you will make yourself unhealthily jealous in the future.

Act in ways that are consistent with your unhealthy jealousy-based irrational beliefs

If you have followed and implemented what I have said so far, you should now be able to make yourself feel unhealthily jealous. The next step is to maintain and even deepen this unhealthy emotion by acting in ways that are consistent with your unhealthy jealousy-based irrational beliefs. As I have noted several times previously in this book, the advantage of engaging in such behaviours is that doing so helps to reinforce and strengthen your conviction (in this case, your unhealthy jealousy-creating irrational beliefs) so engage in as many as you can.

Question your partner constantly and don't accept what they say

Your unhealthy jealousy-related irrational belief will urge you to question your partner about their feelings, thoughts and behaviours, particularly with respect to any love rivals on the horizon. Don't resist this urge. Indeed, make sure that you make use of every opportunity to question your partner on these matters. When they answer your questions, don't believe in the veracity of these responses. Look for any inconsistencies in what your partner says and ask further questions about these inconsistencies.

If they refuse to answer your questions, accuse them of being unfaithful to you. When they deny these accusations, take what they say and ask questions about it. Keep this process going until your partner storms off. When you next see them, say that their storming off proved that they had been unfaithful.

Check on your partner constantly

When you are not in your partner's presence, your unhealthy jealousy-related irrational beliefs will lead you to make checks on their whereabouts. There are a number of ways in which you can do this. You can:

- follow your partner surreptitiously;
- telephone your partner (mobile phones are particularly useful in this respect);
- get reports on your partner's activities from friends (if you are rich you may hire a private investigator).

Your checking behaviours will help you to maintain your unhealthy jealousy by keeping in your mind that there is a threat to your relationship with your partner and that if you don't know what your partner is doing, for example, then they are up to no good. While thinking in these ways, rehearse your irrational beliefs to guarantee the unhealthy jealousy experience.

Monitor your partner closely when in their presence

When you are with your partner, your unhealthy jealousy-based irrational beliefs will lead you to monitor them closely. Do this particularly when in the presence of potential love rivals. Assume further that your partner is looking at one such rival if you see them glancing in the rival's general direction, and further assume that your partner is interested in the rival. Once again, such monitoring will remind you of the idea that threats to your relationship with your partner are everywhere, a key component of unhealthy jealousy.

You can also monitor the behaviour and gaze direction of your potential love rivals and assume that they are interested in your partner, even in the absence of corroborating evidence.

Accuse your partner of indiscretions and infidelities

Your unhealthy jealousy-related irrational beliefs will encourage you to accuse your partner of various indiscretions and infidelities. If you do this frequently, your partner will eventually withdraw from you because they find your behaviour aversive. Use this withdrawal as evidence that they are interested in someone else. Accuse them of this; doing so will help to increase your conviction that threats to your relationship are ubiquitous. Bring your irrational beliefs to this conclusion if you do not do so spontaneously, to perpetuate your unhealthy jealousy.

Set traps for your partner

One of my clients who had a problem with unhealthy jealousy suspected that her husband was interested in other women. So she introduced him to an attractive woman at a works party who she knew delighted in sleeping with other women's husbands. She then left the party, claiming to have a migraine, but insisted that her husband stay and give the woman a lift home. When he came home, she accused him of sleeping with the woman, even though he had had neither the time nor the interest to do so. In short, my client's unhealthy jealousy-based irrational beliefs led her to set a trap for her husband. This only served to reinforce my client's irrational beliefs. The moral of this story is this: if you wish to remain unhealthily jealous, set traps for your partner, assume that they have fallen for the traps and accuse them of being indiscreet or being unfaithful.

Place restrictions on your partner

Another good way of perpetuating your feelings of unhealthy jealousy and the irrational beliefs that underpin these feelings is to place restrictions on your partner which effectively stop them from engaging in activities that you find threatening. For example, if you fear that your partner will talk to and show interest in potential love rivals at social gatherings to which you have not been invited, ban your partner from attending these functions. In doing so you will reinforce your unhealthy jealousy, because by placing restrictions on your partner you are acting according to the following ideas: 'I forbid you to attend social gatherings without me, because if you go I will not know what you are getting up to. I need to know that you are not showing interest in a potential love rival, and because I don't know this I will assume that you are showing a romantic interest in this person. Also, if you do talk to someone that I deem to be a love rival, this means that you prefer them to me and I couldn't stand that.' I recommend that you make such an implicit dialogue explicit to yourself so that you can 'feel' justified in your restrictive behaviour.

Retaliate

Another good way of perpetuating unhealthy jealousy and the unhealthy beliefs that underpin it is to retaliate against your partner's presumed infidelities. I say 'presumed' here because you may have little actual evidence that your partner has been unfaithful to you. This doesn't really matter: what does matter is that you believe that your partner has been unfaithful. Given this, be unfaithful yourself as a way of getting back at your partner. You might even get your retaliation in first and have an affair before you discover that your partner has been unfaithful to you – after all, it is only a matter of time before they do.

Retaliating against your partner (before or after the event) is a way of keeping to the forefront of your mind the notion that there is an ever-present threat to your relationship to which you will easily bring your irrational beliefs to create ever-present unhealthy jealousy.

Punish your partner

Retaliation helps to perpetuate unhealthy jealousy: inherent in the idea of retaliating against your partner is the inference that they have been unfaithful to you (or will inevitably be unfaithful in the future). When you punish your partner you also assume that they have been unfaithful to you in some way, thus strengthening the idea in your mind that threats to your relationship are ubiquitous, which you then evaluate with irrational beliefs. Such punishments are particularly potent when you do not disclose why you are punishing your partner. Here, you will notice some overlap between unhealthy jealousy and feelings of hurt (see Chapter 6), particularly when you punish your partner by refusing to communicate with them (i.e. punishment by sulking). Another popular way of punishing your partner for being unfaithful to you is to verbally berate them. This works particularly well if you cling to the notion that anything they may say in their defence is a lie!

Punish your love rival

Punishing your rival for taking your partner away from you (for this is how you see it in your mind) is another good behavioural way of keeping unhealthy jealousy alive. It does so because it helps you to keep in mind that rivals to your partner's affections are omnipresent and are likely to be successful, and thus it gives you a further opportunity to rehearse your unhealthy jealousy-related irrational beliefs which you easily bring to such eventualities. By the way, if you still find it difficult to think irrationally about threats to your relationship with your partner, you are not trying hard enough. Re-read this chapter – and this time, pay attention! How can you punish your rival? In similar ways that you used when punishing your partner. Attacking them verbally is a particularly good approach in this context.

Develop and rehearse general unhealthy jealousy-based irrational beliefs

The next step in furthering your competence at making yourself unhealthily jealous is for you to develop and rehearse general unhealthy jealousy-based irrational beliefs. General unhealthy jealousy-based irrational beliefs are irrational beliefs that you hold in many theme-related situations that enable you to experience unhealthy jealousy in these situations. If you develop and rehearse such beliefs you will enable yourself to experience unhealthy jealousy in many different situations. You will do this mainly because you will become skilled at inferring that you are facing a threat to your relationship with your partner in the absence of corroborative evidence.

Let me show you how this works. First, you need to develop a general unhealthy jealousy-based irrational belief, such as: 'My partner must only show interest in me and if they show interest in someone else it means that I am unworthy.' Now, if you rehearse this general belief until you firmly believe it and you bring it to relevant situations where it is possible that your partner may show interest in someone else, then because you cannot convince yourself that your partner is not interested in the other person, you will tend to think that they are, and furthermore that the other person is interested in your partner and that they want to begin a relationship with one another. Having created this unhealthy jealousy-based inference, you will then evaluate it using a specific version of this general unhealthy jealousy-based irrational belief, and will thereby make yourself feel unhealthy jealousy in the specific situation.

Let me give you a concrete example of how to do this. Develop the following general unhealthy jealousy-based irrational belief: 'I must know at all times what my partner is doing and it's terrible if I don't know this.' Imagine taking this belief to a specific situation where your partner leaves a message on your answerphone saying that they will be home late from work. Your general unhealthy jealousy-based irrational belief will lead you to infer that your partner is out with a potential love rival. It is as if you reason: 'Because I don't know what my partner is doing and it is terrible not to know, not knowing means that they are with someone else.' Your belief does not readily allow you to think that your partner is doing something completely innocent like working late on their own. Once

111

you have created your inference that your partner is with a love rival, it is fairly easy to make yourself feel unhealthy jealousy about it by evaluating it with a specific related irrational belief, thus: 'My partner is with someone else tonight. This proves that I am worthless.'

Having made yourself feel unhealthy jealousy in this way, the next step is to act and think in ways that are consistent with your unhealthy jealousy and that will strengthen your conviction in your unhealthy jealousy-based irrational belief, increasing the chances that you will perpetuate your unhealthy jealousy problem.

Develop and rehearse a view of the world founded on unhealthy jealousy-based irrational beliefs

I have mentioned several times in this book that people develop world views that render them vulnerable to particular unhealthy negative emotions. The world views that render you vulnerable to unhealthy jealousy do so again because they make it very easy for you to make unhealthy jealousy-related inferences. Then, as I have shown you earlier in this chapter, you make yourself unhealthily jealous about these inferences with the appropriate irrational beliefs. Here is an illustrative list of unhealthy jealousy-related world views for you to develop and rehearse, together with the inferences that they spawn.

World view: Partners will ultimately leave

Inference: My partner is on the look-out for someone better.

World view: Partners are basically untrustworthy

Inference: Whatever my partner says about her feelings towards me and love rivals is not to be taken at face value.

World view: If I trust someone they will make a fool of me, so I need to always be on my guard

Inference: When my partner asks me to trust him, he is up to no good.

World view: Not knowing what partners are feeling, thinking and doing is very dangerous

If I don't know what my partner is feeling, thinking or doing, this means that they are interested in someone else and/or thinking of leaving me.

I hope you can see how you can become really adept at creating unhealthy jealousy for yourself. I will now move on to teach you how to become really adept at making yourself feel unhealthy envy.

8

How to Make Yourself
Feel Unhealthily Envious

Unhealthy envy is a particularly destructive emotion. It can sour your relationships and lead you to become obsessed with what you don't have in life, leaving you to take for granted or neglect what you do have. As we will see, it can also lead you to destroy or spoil what others have.

Before I teach you how to make yourself unhealthily envious, I need once again to discuss terminology. As with anger and jealousy, we don't have very good words to discriminate between unhealthy and healthy envy, so I will use these two terms here. Of course, my goal is to teach you how to make yourself unhealthily envious, not healthily so. By *unhealthy envy*, I mean a state where you demand that you must have what you covet in others' lives. Your inclination is to aim to get what you lack at all costs, or, if not, to spoil or destroy things for others. By contrast, *healthy envy* is a state where you would like to have what you covet in others' lives, but don't demand that you must get it. Your inclination is to strive for what you want as long as it is healthy to do so, and you have no desire to spoil or destroy things for others.

As you can see, healthy envy is far too constructive a response and should be avoided at all costs. If you follow the advice that follows, you will be able to avoid feeling healthily envious.

How to make yourself unhealthily envious: general steps

The steps that you need to take to make yourself unhealthily envious will be well known to you by now, but I will review them for the last time as they apply to unhealthy envy.

1 Make an inference about what you are focusing on.
2 Appraise that inference using unhealthy envy-based irrational beliefs.
3 Think in ways that are consistent with the above irrational beliefs.
4 Act in ways that are consistent with these irrational beliefs.

115

5 Develop and rehearse a general version of your specific unhealthy envy-based irrational beliefs so that you can become skilled at making unhealthy envy-based inferences about what is generally going on in your life.

6 Develop and rehearse an unhealthy envy-based world view.

I will now deal with these issues one at a time.

Make unhealthy envy-related inferences

To feel unhealthily envious, focus on a scenario (which can be real or imagined) which usually has three elements to it: you, another person (or people) and something or someone that the other has that you prize but that you do not have. Envy is often confused with jealousy, which, as I showed you in the previous chapter, involves you thinking that you face a threat to your relationship with your partner. I often explain the difference in the following way. I am bald and I would like to have a full head of hair. Now, imagine that I meet a man with a full head of hair. If I were envious of the person's hair, I would be saying that I would like to have a full head of hair like him. If I were jealous of the person's hair I would be saying that I think that the person's hair (not the person himself) poses a threat to my relationship with my partner – clearly a ridiculous notion.

Here are a number of envy scenarios to show the range of things you can envy. It is important to bear in mind that you may be envious of a specific object that another may have, for example, or something like that specific object. This is the case with all cases of envy.

- Barry was envious of his friend's attractive wife (object of envy: a person).
- Linda was envious of her friend's good looks (object of envy: physical characteristics).
- Muriel was envious of her married friends' family life (object of envy: family life).
- Phil was envious of his friend's promotion (object of envy: achievement).
- Mr and Mrs Smith were envious of their friends' lavish lifestyle (object of envy: lifestyle).
- Ben was envious of his friend's extraversion (object of envy: personal characteristic).

116

- Jane was envious of Beryl's ability to play the piano (object of envy: talent).
- Bill was envious of his friend's Porsche (object of envy: possession).

As I have mentioned several times before in this book, these inferences do not have to reflect reality. This doesn't matter too much, for the important point is that you have to believe that they are true.

Hold and rehearse irrational beliefs about your unhealthy envy-related inference

Your unhealthy envy is not caused by your inference that another person has something that you want but that you don't have. Rather, these unhealthy feelings are determined by the irrational beliefs that you hold about this inference, true or not. So let me teach you how to feel unhealthily envious by detailing which irrational beliefs to develop and rehearse about the above inferences.

There are, in fact, two different types of unhealthy envy, ego envy and non-ego envy, although you may have both.

Unhealthy ego envy

In ego envy you tend to invest your self-esteem in whatever it is that others have that you want but don't have. In order to make yourself unhealthily envious in the ego domain, you need to hold two irrational beliefs:

- a rigid demand (e.g. 'A colleague got promoted and I absolutely should get promoted as well');
- a self-depreciation belief (e.g. 'I am less worthy than my colleague for not getting promoted').

Unhealthy non-ego envy

In non-ego envy, you disturb yourself about not having what you want. You do not invest your self-esteem in whatever you don't have. In order to make yourself unhealthily envious in the non-ego domain, you need to hold two irrational beliefs:

- a rigid demand (e.g. 'A colleague got promoted and I absolutely should get promoted as well');

- a low frustration tolerance (LFT) belief (e.g. 'I can't stand the situation where my colleague got promoted and I didn't').

The importance of focus in unhealthy envy and the impact on irrational beliefs

So far I have taught you how to feel unhealthy envy when the focus is on you wanting what someone else has and then evaluating this situation with your irrational beliefs. You can also change the focus so that it is on you wanting someone else not to have what you don't have, and then making yourself unhealthily envious about this state of affairs. Let's take the example I have just discussed, where a work colleague has just been promoted and you haven't. I have shown you how to make yourself unhealthily envious by believing 'I must get promoted like my colleague', but you can also make yourself unhealthily envious by changing the focus of the situation so that you believe 'My colleague absolutely should not have been promoted when I didn't.'

Let me now illustrate the above by returning to the examples I outlined earlier. I will assume that in all the scenarios the envy experienced was unhealthy in nature.

- Barry was unhealthily envious of his friend's attractive wife (object of envy: a person).

Barry's unhealthy envy was largely non-ego in nature. He thus held the following irrational beliefs: 'I must have an attractive wife like my friend has and I can't stand not having one.'

- Linda was unhealthily envious of her friend's good looks (object of envy: physical characteristics).

Linda's unhealthy envy was largely ego in nature. She held the following irrational beliefs: 'I must be as attractive as my friend and I am less worthy than her because I am not.'

(This example shows the comparative aspect of envy, as Linda is judging herself to be less worthy than her friend because she considers herself to be less attractive than the other.)

- Muriel was envious of her married friends' family life (object of envy: family life).

Muriel's unhealthy envy was both ego and non-ego in nature. She believed the following: 'I must have a family like my friends do. Not having what I want in this regard is intolerable (non-ego) and proves that I am unlovable (ego).'

- Phil was envious of his friend's promotion (object of envy: achievement).

Phil's unhealthy envy was largely ego in nature. He held the following irrational beliefs: 'My friend absolutely should not have been promoted when I wasn't. The fact that he was and I wasn't proves that I am a rotten person.'

- Mr and Mrs Smith were envious of their friends' lavish lifestyle (object of envy: lifestyle).

Mr and Mrs Smith's unhealthy envy was largely non-ego in nature and was based on the following shared irrational beliefs: 'Our friends must not have the lifestyle that we don't have and we can't stand it that they do and we don't.'

- Ben was envious of his friend's extraversion (object of envy: personal characteristic).

Ben's unhealthy envy was largely ego in nature. He believed the following: 'I must be more outgoing like my friend. The fact that I am not proves that he is a better person than I am.'

- Jane was envious of Beryl's ability to play the piano (object of envy: talent).

Jane's unhealthy envy was both ego and non-ego in nature. She held the following irrational beliefs: 'Beryl must not be able to play the piano better than me. I can't bear the fact that I don't have her talent (non-ego) and because I don't this proves that she is worthier than me (ego).'

- Bill was envious of his friend's Porsche (object of envy: possession).

Bill's unhealthy envy was largely non-ego in nature. He held the following irrational beliefs: 'My friend must not have a Porsche when I don't have one. I can't bear the fact that he has what I don't have.'

Think in ways that are consistent with your unhealthy envy-based irrational beliefs

When you hold an unhealthy envy-creating irrational belief, this belief will influence the way that you subsequently think. If you practise these forms of thinking then you will develop your ability to make yourself unhealthily envious, particularly by strengthening your conviction in your irrational belief. So when you begin to experience unhealthy envy, think in a number of distorted ways.

Before I discuss these ways of thinking, let me stress an important point about unhealthy envy. At the heart of unhealthy envy is an intolerance of being in a disadvantaged position. Some instances of unhealthy envy are about making things equal. In one such case, you are content (albeit for a short period) when you get what you covet in the life of others. Here, you are not concerned if others have it as long as you have it. In the other case, if you don't have whatever it is that you covet in the life of others, your object is to deprive them of what you covet, to spoil it for them or to destroy it. You are content (again albeit for a short period) that they don't have what you don't have.

Related to unhealthy envy (but not strictly speaking envy, since it does not involve you being in a situation where you covet something belonging to someone else) is resentment about having to share what you covet. Here, you seek to put yourself in an advantaged position and the other in a disadvantaged position. You are not content to have what you covet if others have it too. You will only be content (in a disturbed sense) if you have it and others don't. Thus, you must get what you demand and make sure that others don't have it. Needless to say, this is quite destructive and elements of this thinking are found in the thinking consequences of some unhealthy envy-related irrational beliefs. Remember these points as you learn how to perpetuate your unhealthy envy by making your subsequent thinking distorted, as in the following ways:

Think obsessively about how to get what you envy regardless of its usefulness

When you are unhealthily envious and you demand that you must get what the other person has that you lack, you will find it easy to become obsessed with whatever it is that you covet but don't have, and you will think obsessively about getting whatever it is that you covet, regardless of its usefulness to you and regardless of the price you may have to pay (financially and psychologically) in order to get it. In other words, such obsessive thinking flows fairly naturally from your unhealthy envy-based irrational beliefs. However, if your thinking isn't obsessive in nature, you can give it a push, so to speak, in the obsessive direction by focusing on what you don't have and repeating to yourself that it is absolutely essential to get it. Also, devise as many plans as you can think of to help you get what you now think of as crucial to your life. Obsessive thinking will soon 'kick in' and have the added benefit of strengthening your need-based irrational beliefs that have led to you feeling unhealthily envious in the first place.

Think about depriving the other person of what you envy

If your unhealthy envy-based irrational belief is centred on others not having what you don't have, you can strengthen this belief by thinking about what you can do to deprive the other person of what they have that you covet. Picture yourself taking whatever it is away from them and focus on the pleasure you experience by so depriving them. As you do so, justify your actions by telling yourself that you are righting a wrong. After all, it is dreadfully unfair if the other person has what you don't have, and you are just making an unfair situation fair by depriving them of what you covet.

On the other hand, if you are intent on keeping whatever it is that you have deprived them of, picture yourself keeping it and justify yourself by showing how much you deserve to have whatever it is that you have coveted.

Think about spoiling or destroying what you envy so that the other doesn't have it

If you can't deprive the other person of the object of your unhealthy envy, you can always make things equal in your mind by having thoughts and images of spoiling or destroying what the other has that you unhealthily covet. Again, as you fantasize about spoiling or destroying the other's possession, for example, focus on the pleasure that you get from doing so and don't forget to justify your behaviour to yourself.

Think obsessively of how to get what you covet and how to deprive the other person or spoil or destroy the object of your unhealthy envy for others

Here, you combine the thinking consequences discussed above. This cocktail is particularly potent in perpetuating your unhealthy envy-related irrational beliefs.

Think denigrating thoughts about the person who has what you envy

One way of making things equal in your mind when you are feeling unhealthily envious is to denigrate in your mind the person who has what you envy. For example, if they have a possession that you

121

covet, put them down by telling yourself that they are greedy or that they are too ignorant to appreciate what they have. Thinking this way will strengthen your conviction in your unhealthy envy-related beliefs and thus increase the probability that you will experience unhealthy envy in the future.

Think denigrating thoughts about what you envy

A similar equalizing mental technique is to denigrate in your mind what you envy. This is the 'sour grapes' mentality. Thus, if you covet the grapes that your friend has that you don't have, tell yourself that these grapes are probably sour. This will help you to feel better and to get better at making yourself feel unhealthily envious in the first place.

Try to convince yourself that you are happy with what you have and that you don't really desire what you envy

Another way of making things equal in your mind is to attempt to convince yourself that you are happy with what you have and that you don't really want what you do in reality envy. Thus, if you covet your friend's grapes (and hold unhealthy envy-related irrational beliefs about this situation), try to make things equal in your mind by attempting to convince yourself that the banana that you have is all that you really want.

You can, of course, combine this strategy with the previous one and attempt to show yourself that not only is your banana all that you really want, but that your friend's grapes are in all probability sour.

Deny that you feel unhealthily envious

A number of the above thinking strategies involve you lying to yourself. This serves to perpetuate your unhealthy envy-related irrational beliefs, in that you not only embellish these beliefs but also protect them from investigation, and therefore change, by in effect denying that you feel unhealthily envious in the first place. A stark and successful example of this is outright denial to yourself that you do in fact feel unhealthily envious, or telling yourself that your envy is really healthy. An example of the former is to tell yourself: 'No, I really don't want that' (when you really do), and an example of the latter is to tell yourself: 'Yes, I would like that, but I don't need it' (when in reality you do believe that you really need it). If you can

122

delude yourself in these ways then this will definitely help you to keep your unhealthy envy-based irrational beliefs alive, thus giving you hours, days, months and even years of delicious unhealthy envy to look forward to.

Act in ways that are consistent with your unhealthy envy-based irrational beliefs

If you have followed and implemented what I have said so far, you should now be able to make yourself feel unhealthily envious. The next step is to maintain and even deepen this unhealthy emotion by acting in ways that are consistent with your unhealthy envy-based irrational beliefs. As I have noted several times previously in this book, the advantage of engaging in such behaviours is that doing so helps to reinforce and strengthen your conviction (in this case, your unhealthy envy-creating irrational beliefs), so engage in as many as you can. Many of these behaviours are active expressions of the thinking consequences discussed above, and for best effect you need to tailor them to meet your individual requirements.

Seek out what you envy, whether you really want it or not

Once you have identified the object of your unhealthy envy, devote all your time and efforts to pursuing it whether or not it is healthy to do so and whether or not it is really what you want. The more obsessive–compulsive you can become in your pursuit of the object of your envy, the better. Such obsessive–compulsive striving will reinforce your unhealthy envy-based irrational beliefs.

Once you get what you envy, put it to one side and look around for something else that you envy

If you are successful in getting what you envy, put it to one side and look around for something else that you covet which you don't have and others do, and then strive obsessively–compulsively for this new envy object while, of course, rehearsing your unhealthy envy-based irrational beliefs. Continue this pattern until it becomes second nature to you.

It is important to put your envy object to one side once you have achieved it, so that you reinforce the idea that what is essential to you is to get rid of the deprivation of not having what you think you must have rather than enjoying the envy object itself.

Other unhealthy envy-based irrational belief behavioural maintainers

The following involve behavioural expressions of the thinking strategies discussed above:

- Actively attempt to take away what you envy from the other.
- Actively attempt to spoil or destroy what you envy that the other has.
- Verbally disparage the person who has what you envy.
- Verbally disparage what you envy to others.
- Tell others that you don't really want what you envy.

Don't forget to rehearse your specific unhealthy envy-based irrational beliefs while carrying out these behaviours, particularly if you think that you are becoming healthily envious, something which you should actively strive to avoid.

Develop and rehearse general unhealthy envy-based irrational beliefs

The next step in furthering your competence at making yourself unhealthily envious is developing and rehearsing general unhealthy envy-based irrational beliefs. General unhealthy envy-based irrational beliefs are irrational beliefs that you hold in many theme-related situations; they enable you to experience unhealthy envy in these situations. If you develop and rehearse such beliefs, you will enable yourself to experience unhealthy envy in many different situations. You will do this mainly because you will become skilled at focusing on what you covet in the life of others that you don't have. For, once you believe that you must have what you covet in the life of others, you will focus on what you don't have and edit out what you do have. Once you have identified a specific envy object in this way, evaluate it with a specific variant of your general unhealthy envy-based irrational belief so that you make yourself unhealthily envious in this situation.

Having made yourself feel unhealthily envious in this way, the next step is to act and think in ways that are consistent with your unhealthy envy and that will strengthen your conviction in your unhealthy envy-based irrational belief, increasing the chances that you will perpetuate your unhealthy envy problem.

Develop and rehearse a view of the world founded on unhealthy envy-based irrational beliefs

I have mentioned several times in this book that people develop world views that render them vulnerable to particular unhealthy negative emotions. The world views that render you vulnerable to unhealthy envy do so because they make it very easy for you to focus on what you don't have (and covet) and edit out in your mind what you do have. Then, as I have shown you earlier in this chapter, you make yourself unhealthily envious about this situation, with the appropriate irrational beliefs. Here is an illustrative list of unhealthy envy-related world views for you to develop and rehearse, together with the inferences that they spawn.

World view: The grass is always greener in the lives of others
Inference: Whatever I have is less attractive than what others have.

World view: Satisfaction can only be achieved if I get what I want
Inference: If I get what I covet it will satisfy me.
(This, of course, is a delusion, since unhealthy envy-related irrational beliefs render you insatiable.)

World view: It's unfair if others have what I don't have, but it is fair if I have what others don't have
Inference: If I don't have something I covet that someone has, this inequality is unfair.

World view: People's worth is defined by what they have in life
Inference: People will like me for having what I don't have rather than for who I am.

World view: The more I have, the happier I'll be
Inference: In any situation, it is better to have what I don't have than to be content with what I do have.

I hope you can see how you can become really adept at creating unhealthy envy for yourself. In the final chapter, I will give you general advice on how to maintain your emotional disturbance once you have created it.

9

How to Maintain Emotional Disturbance: Some Concluding Advice

In each of the foregoing chapters, I have taken a particular disturbed emotion and given you helpful advice concerning how to make yourself disturbed in the first place and how to perpetuate your disturbance in the second place. In this closing chapter, I will give you some brief advice concerning how to maintain emotional disturbance generally.

Develop and practise a general philosophy of emotional disturbance

Perhaps the most effective way of maintaining emotional disturbance is to develop and practise what I can best describe as a general philosophy of emotional disturbance. This philosophy comprises four irrational beliefs, and I suggest that you practise these beliefs as follows:

Demanding beliefs
In order to implement demanding beliefs, take your preferences and turn these into absolute demands. As a person, it's likely that you have three main preferences:

- preferences about self (e.g. 'I want to be approved', 'I want to succeed');
- preferences about others (e.g. 'I want you to be kind');
- preferences about life conditions (e.g. 'I want life to be just').

Then take these desires and make them rigid by turning them into absolute demands. Thus:

- demands about self (e.g. 'I must be approved', 'I must succeed');
- demands about others (e.g. 'You must be kind');
- demands about life conditions (e.g. 'Life must be just').

Then apply these general demands to specific situations and you will enjoy endless hours of emotional disturbance.

Awfulizing beliefs

In order to implement awfulizing beliefs, focus generally on what you consider to be bad in life and then make your evaluations extreme. Tell yourself, for example, 'It will be the end of the world if I don't succeed', 'It's terrible that you weren't kind' or 'It's awful if life is not just.' Then apply these general awfulizing beliefs to specific situations whenever you encounter what is bad in life.

Low frustration tolerance (LFT) beliefs

In order to implement LFT beliefs, focus on whatever you find difficult to tolerate in life. Then tell yourself that you can't bear it and that it is not worth bearing, even though in reality it is.

Depreciation beliefs

You can hold depreciation beliefs about yourself, other people or life conditions. In order to implement depreciation beliefs, focus on something negative about yourself, another person or life conditions, and then give yourself, the other person or life conditions a global negative rating on the basis of that negative aspect. Thus:

- 'I am worthless for failing.'
- 'You are no good for treating people unkindly.'
- 'Life is no good for not giving me what I deserve.'

Then apply these beliefs to relevant specific events.

In order to make your general philosophy of emotional disturbance really work for you, you need to think and act in ways that are consistent with the four irrational beliefs that comprise this philosophy. I have given many different examples of how to do this in the previous chapters. Once you have understood this principle you can use it to keep your emotional disturbance going indefinitely.

Deny to yourself that you have emotional disturbance

Once you have made yourself emotionally disturbed, a good way of perpetuating it is to deny to yourself that you have it. To do this successfully, you need to knowingly practise what I have taught you in this book, i.e. to disturb yourself and then to deny to yourself that you have done this.

If you can do this, then successful denial means that since you do not acknowledge that you feel disturbed you have no need to do anything constructive about it. Doing nothing constructive about your emotional disturbance will lead to its perpetuation.

Don't take responsibility for your emotional disturbance

If you cannot successfully delude yourself that you do not feel emotionally disturbed when you actually do, then don't despair; there is another way of allowing yourself to remain disturbed. It involves you not taking responsibility for your emotional disturbance. There are a number of ways that you can refrain from taking such responsibility. Here are some examples:

- Blame your parents (e.g. 'My parents have made me anxious and insecure').
- Blame your genes (e.g. 'I'm a born worrier. Always have been, always will be. It's in my genes').
- Blame your past environment (e.g. 'I grew up in a family in which nobody expressed how they felt. That's why I'm scared of conflict today').
- Blame your present environment (e.g. 'The uncertainty at work causes my panic').
- Blame past experiences (e.g. 'I was bullied at school. That caused me to be scared of people').
- Blame present experiences (e.g. 'Being made redundant has made me depressed').

There is an element of truth to all these statements, in that all the above-mentioned factors do contribute to your current emotional disturbance. However, in reality they do not cause your disturbed feelings, which are largely determined by your irrational beliefs about events. Indeed, I have devoted considerable space in this book to teaching you how to make yourself emotionally disturbed by developing and practising such irrational beliefs.

So, on the one hand you need to practise disturbing yourself by rehearsing such irrational beliefs, while on the other hand you need to refrain from taking responsibility for creating such disturbance by blaming outside events, other people, your environment and your genes for your disturbance. Refraining from taking responsibility for your disturbed feelings means that you will not do anything to change them, which in effect means that you will maintain them.

Disturb yourself about your disturbances

A particularly effective way of perpetuating your emotional disturbance involves you disturbing yourself about your emotional disturbances. Not only is this an effective way of maintaining a particular emotional problem, it has the added advantage of giving you a second emotional problem: two problems for the price of one!

There are two major ways of giving yourself a meta-emotional problem (an emotional problem about an emotional problem). First, you can do so in the ego domain (e.g. 'I must not get myself unhealthily angry and if I do this it proves that I am an inadequate person'), and second, you can do so in the non-ego domain (e.g. 'I must not get myself unhealthily angry. I can't bear the experience of feeling unhealthily angry').

Another way of addressing the topic of making yourself disturbed about your emotional disturbance is to make a list of the eight disturbed emotions discussed in this book and consider how you can disturb yourself about these emotions using emotions from the same list. Here are some examples, with their associated irrational beliefs:

- anxiety about anxiety (e.g. 'I must not feel anxious and if I do it would be unbearable');
- shame about unhealthy envy (e.g. 'I must not show that I am unhealthily envious and if I do it proves that I am a disgusting person');
- guilt about the expression of unhealthy anger (e.g. 'I must not show my unhealthy anger and if I do it proves that I am a bad person');
- depression about depression (e.g. 'I must not make myself depressed and if I do it proves that I am a weak, inadequate person');
- anxiety about hurt (e.g. 'I must not feel hurt and if I do I won't be able to stand it').

Focus on the payoffs of being emotionally disturbed and the costs of being psychologically healthy

Sometimes you may forget the advantages of emotional disturbance and may be tempted to overcome your emotional problems. Be on your guard and resist such temptation. Instead, remind yourself of all the payoffs that stem from being emotionally disturbed and the costs of being psychologically healthy. If you find yourself struggling to do this, the following list, which I first presented in the Introduction, may help you.

Payoffs for being emotionally disturbed

- You get sympathy from people.
- People will help you out with a variety of tasks.
- You can get time off from work and still get paid.
- You may get early retirement on health grounds and get your pension paid early.
- People won't ask you to do difficult tasks.
- People won't put you under stress, so you will have an easier life.
- People won't have high expectations of you.
- You may be able to get people to do what you want them to do by reminding them verbally or by your actions that you suffer from emotional disturbance.
- Some people will look after you.
- If you are a student you may be able to get your degree without doing any work by dint of being emotionally disturbed.
- If you fail at anything then you can put the blame on the fact that you were emotionally disturbed ('It wasn't me, it was my illness').

Costs of being psychologically healthy

- People will expect much of you and will be disappointed in you if you fail to live up to their expectations.
- You will be expected to carry the workload of others who are off sick (including those who are away from work due to psychological problems).
- People will ask you to do onerous tasks because they think you are healthy enough to cope with them.
- You will get little sympathy from people if you show how emotionally healthy you are.

131

- People will expect you to look after them. They will certainly not want to look after you.
- Few people will offer to help you with things.
- If you do fail at anything you will not have anything or anyone to blame for this but yourself.
- People will not make allowances for you.

I hope you can see from the above that being emotionally disturbed leads to an easier life and being psychologically healthy leads to a much harder life.

Now compile your own list of payoffs for being emotionally disturbed and costs of being psychologically healthy, and review this list if you are ever tempted to overcome your emotional problems.

Make and act on self-fulfilling prophecies

Quite a good way of maintaining your emotional disturbance is to construct and act on self-fulfilling prophecies. Here is an example of a self-fulfilling prophecy. Let's suppose that you have made yourself disturbed by developing and rehearsing the following irrational belief: 'I must do well socially and I am an inadequate person if I don't.' This irrational belief has produced the following unhealthy consequences:

- emotional consequences: anxiety, shame;
- behavioural consequences: avoidance of social situations, withdrawal from social situations;
- thinking consequences: 'Nobody will want to talk to me if I go out', 'If people talk to me they will think that I am strange.'

Now, let's suppose that you have been invited to go to a party and you are unable to get out of going. Going to the party is problematic because it may challenge some of the above ideas: somebody may want to talk to you, and if they do they may not think that you are strange. So, in order to avoid the possibility of a positive experience leading to psychological health, take the following steps, which constitute the development and implementation of a self-fulfilling belief.

1 Take one of your thinking consequences and tailor it to the specific situation you are about to face (e.g. 'When I go to the party nobody will talk to me').
2 Act in a way to bring about this result (e.g. don't talk to anyone and make it difficult for anybody to talk to you. For example, avoid all eye contact, and grunt or don't reply at all if anyone does talk to you).
3 When you have achieved this result use it to determine the accuracy of your original prediction and as evidence for the accuracy of your irrational belief (e.g. 'You see I was right all along. I went to the party and nobody spoke to me. This proves that I am an inadequate person').
4 Don't take any responsibility for bringing about the result that you predicted (e.g. on no account acknowledge that your behaviour actively discouraged people from talking to you).

Practise the above steps until you become competent at maintaining your disturbance by constructing and implementing self-fulfilling prophecies. You won't regret it!

Develop blocks to personal change

If for any reason you find yourself in a situation where you may be tempted to do something to overcome your emotional problems (and I certainly hope that you never find yourself in this situation), it is useful to come up with a number of reasons why you can't or won't change. Furthermore, I suggest that you write down and review such blocks to personal change so that you can effectively resist any urges that you may experience to help yourself. The following is a list of such blocks that may help stimulate your thinking on the matter:

- I'm too old to change.
- I'm too set in my ways to change.
- I have held my irrational beliefs for too long to change them now.
- Personal change is too hard.
- Personal change will be too disruptive to my life.
- I'm too lazy to change.
- I fail at everything I do, so there's no point me trying to change since I'm bound to fail.

- Other people need to change, I don't.
- It's unfair that I suffer from emotional disturbance when others don't, therefore I absolutely shouldn't have to work hard to change myself.
- I'm used to who I am. If I changed I wouldn't know who I was.
- My past has irrevocably damaged me, so change is not possible.
- My emotional disturbance is inherited so I can't do anything to help myself; my problems are in my genes.

Complain endlessly to people about your problems and use the 'yes ... but' technique when given encouragement and helpful advice

Another good way of resisting personal change and helping to maintain your emotional disturbance is to complain endlessly about things you are disturbed about and negate any constructive help and encouragement you may get from the other person. This involves using the 'yes ... but' technique. When you use this technique, you seem to agree with the person's advice or you seem to respond constructively to their encouragement (i.e. 'yes ...'), and then you show why you can't take the advice or why the encouragement is misplaced (i.e. 'but ...').

Here is an illustrative dialogue to demonstrate how you can perpetuate your emotional disturbance by complaining and resisting change using the 'yes ... but' technique.

You: I'm too scared to apply for that job that you told me about.
Friend: You've got no reason to be scared, you could do that job blindfold.
You: It's kind of you to say so, but technology has moved on a lot since I last worked in the field.
Friend: But you're bright and you could easily update yourself on those developments.
You: Yes, that may have been the case once, but I've lost my confidence.
Friend: Your confidence will come back if you take the risk and do things unconfidently for a while.
You: Yes, that would have probably been the case when I was younger, but now I'm older I can't do that.
Friend: Wow, you are really down on yourself. I suggest that you see a counsellor.
You: Yes, that's a good idea, but I can't afford to.

Friend: I'll lend you the money.
You: That's very kind of you, but I hate borrowing money from anyone.
Friend: OK. I'll pay for the counselling.
You: That's enormously kind of you, but that will put me under too much pressure to change and I really feel that I can't change.

An added bonus of using the complaining 'yes . . . but' combination is that you will eventually alienate your friends. If this happens, you can always complain about it to others and eventually alienate them by consistent application of the 'yes . . . but' technique.

Develop doubts, reservations and objections to a philosophy of psychological health

The final way of maintaining your emotional disturbance that I want to discuss involves you taking the healthy alternative to your general disturbance-creating philosophy that I discussed at the beginning of this chapter and constructing a number of doubts, reservations and objections to what might be called a philosophy of psychological health. Before I help you to come up with such doubts, reservations and objections, let me briefly outline the four rational beliefs that comprise this healthy philosophy. Before I do so, let me state for the record that I am not recommending that you adopt these rational beliefs. Rather, I am listing them so that you can learn how to resist them by coming up with doubts, reservations and objections.

Full preference beliefs

In order to implement full preference beliefs, assert what you want (partial preferences) and negate the demand that you may have developed if you have followed my advice throughout this book. As a person, it's likely that you will have three main partial preferences:

- partial preferences about self (e.g. 'I want to be approved', 'I want to succeed');
- partial preferences about others (e.g. 'I want you to be kind');
- partial preferences about life conditions (e.g. 'I want life to be just').

Then take these partial preferences and keep them flexible by refraining from turning them into absolute demands. These are full preferences. Thus:

- full preferences about self (e.g. 'I want to be approved, but I don't have to be', 'I want to succeed, but I don't have to do so');
- full preferences about others (e.g. 'I want you to be kind, but there is no reason why you have to be kind');
- full preferences about life conditions (e.g. 'I want life to be just, but it doesn't have to be just').

Anti-awfulizing beliefs

In order to implement anti-awfulizing beliefs, focus generally on what you consider to be bad in life and then negate the extreme evaluations that I taught you to construct earlier in this book. Tell yourself, for example, 'It will be bad if I don't succeed, but it won't be the end of the world', 'It's unfortunate that you weren't kind, but it's not terrible' or 'It's bad if life is not just, but it is not awful.'

High frustration tolerance (HFT) beliefs

In order to implement HFT beliefs, focus on whatever you find difficult to tolerate in life and then tell yourself that you can bear it and that it is worth bearing.

Acceptance beliefs

You can hold acceptance beliefs about yourself, other people or life conditions. In order to implement acceptance beliefs, focus on something negative about yourself, another person or life conditions and then refrain from giving yourself, the other person or life conditions a global negative rating on the basis of that negative aspect. Rather, show yourself that you and the other person are complex, fallible human beings comprising many good, bad and neutral aspects, who can legitimately rate such aspects of themselves but cannot legitimately give themselves a global rating. Similarly, show yourself that life conditions are made up of many good, bad and neutral features and cannot legitimately be given a global rating. Thus:

- 'I am not worthless for failing. I am a fallible human being, who has failed this time but who is capable of achieving success and failure.'

- 'You are a fallible human being and are not worthless for treating people unkindly, but you have acted badly when you treat people in this way.'
- 'When life does not give me what I deserve it is bad in this respect, but it is not bad in its entirety. Life is a complex mixture of good, bad and neutral features.'

Then apply these beliefs to relevant specific events.

Now, in order to resist acquiring such healthy, rational beliefs it is important that you raise in your mind – and communicate to others if necessary – your doubts, reservations, and objections to these rational beliefs. Here are a few examples to get you thinking about the subject. Compile a written list of such doubts, reservations and objections, and refer to it whenever necessary. If you are engaged in a debate about these reservations, use the 'yes . . . but' technique (described earlier) to maintain your conviction in your unhealthy, irrational beliefs and to get the other person off your back.

- 'Adopting full preferences means losing my motivation. Demands are motivating.'
- 'Adopting full preferences means taking on a ''don't care'' attitude. Demands prove that I care.'
- 'Some things really are awful. Adopting anti-awfulizing beliefs means that I am persuading myself that what is awful really isn't.'
- 'Adopting anti-awfulizing beliefs means I am condoning bad things.'
- 'Adopting HFT beliefs means that I will put up with being treated badly.'
- 'Adopting HFT beliefs means lying to myself that I can stand what I really can't, since many things in life are truly intolerable.'
- 'Adopting self-acceptance beliefs means that I resign myself to being who I am.'
- 'Adopting other-acceptance beliefs means condoning the very bad things that people do to one another.'

Now you have the idea, you can add many more of your own doubts, reservations and objections to this list.

You have reached the end of this book and should now be quite competent at making yourself emotionally disturbed and keeping yourself that way. However, a word of warning. Unless you keep practising the skills of acquiring and maintaining emotional disturbance, you may find yourself lapsing back into psychological health. Guard against this tendency by practising the skills described in this book for at least 30 minutes a day. Remember: 'Practice makes disturbance.' Happy misery!

Index